OXFORD IB PREPARED

BUSINESS MANAGEMENT

2ND EDITION

IB DIPLOMA PROGRAMME

Loykie Lominé

OXFORD
UNIVERSITY PRESS

Great Clarendon Street, Oxford, OX2 6DP, United Kingdom

Oxford University Press is a department of the University of Oxford.

It furthers the University's objective of excellence in research, scholarship, and education by publishing worldwide. Oxford is a registered trade mark of Oxford University Press in the UK and in certain other countries

British Library Cataloguing in Publication Data
Data available

978-1-38-204304-5

10 9 8 7 6 5 4 3 2

Paper used in the production of this book is a natural, recyclable product made from wood grown in sustainable forests.

The manufacturing process conforms to the environmental regulations of the country of origin.

Printed in China by Shanghai Offset Printing Products Ltd

Acknowledgements
The publisher would like to thank the following for permissions to use copyright material:

Cover photo: Liyao Xie/Getty Images

Artworks: QBS Learning

Photos: **p1**: Bernhard Richter/Shutterstock; **p20**: Rawpixel.com/Shutterstock; **p42**: Thanwa photo/Shutterstock; **p69**: Herr Petroff/Shutterstock; **p91**: Anton Veselov/Shutterstock; **p127 (B)**: SK Design / Shutterstock; **p127 (T, M)**: iMoStudio / Shutterstock; **p110**, **p115**, **p132** & **p137**: Liyao Xie/Getty Images.

Although we have made every effort to trace and contact all copyright holders before publication this has not been possible in all cases. If notified, the publisher will rectify any errors or omissions at the earliest opportunity.

Contents

 Answers to questions and exam papers in this book can be found on your free support website. Access the support website here: www.oxfordsecondary.com/ib-prepared-support

INTRODUCTION

This book provides coverage of the IB diploma syllabus in business management and offers support to students preparing for their assessments. The book will help you revise the study material (including all tools and formulae), consolidate your knowledge of the essential terms and concepts, understand the assessment criteria and improve your approach to IB examinations. All topics are illustrated by annotated examples of student answers to sample examination questions, explaining why and how marks may be achieved or missed.

DP business management assessment

Standard Level (SL) and Higher Level (HL) students share two elements of assessment: the **internal assessment** (IA – see page 110), and the **paper 1** exam.

- SL students have another exam, **paper 2**, with a quantitative focus.

- HL students have two other exams, **paper 2**, with a quantitative focus, and **paper 3**, about a social enterprise.

The internal and external assessment marks are combined, as shown in the following table, to give your overall DP business management grade, from 1 (lowest) to 7 (highest).

Assessment overview

Assessment	SL		HL	
	Task	Weight	Task	Weight
IA	Business research project	30%	Business research project	20%
Paper 1	1h30mn exam	35%	1h30mn exam	25%
Paper 2	1h30mn exam	35%	1h45mn exam	30%
Paper 3	–	–	1h15mn exam	25%

Overview of the book structure

The book is composed of several elements.

Five **units**, as in the IB DP business management syllabus:

- Unit 1: Introduction to business management

- Unit 2: Human resource management

- Unit 3: Finance and accounts

- Unit 4: Marketing

- Unit 5: Operations management

Each unit is divided into sub-units with summaries of the key syllabus content and useful content links.

Further sections:

- Internal assessment: explaining the task, the assessment criteria, with tips to avoid common mistakes.

- External assessment: covering paper 1, paper 2 and paper 3 (including evaluative questions worth 10 marks, as paper 1 and paper 2 have one such question worth 10 marks). Examples of IB style practice questions, written exclusively for this book, will give you the opportunity to test yourself before the actual exam, as they provide additional practice problems for the material featured in all the units. The answers and solutions are given online at: **www.oxfordsecondary.com/ib-prepared-support**.

- Business management formulae: containing all of the formulae that you need to know for the exams, notably the ones that are not in the formulae sheet given at the start of the exams.

- Business management toolkit: an additional resource containing all business management tools, with explanations for each about how to use it and what to bear in mind.

Concepts

The following four concepts underpin the DP business management course:

- Change
- Creativity
- Ethics
- Sustainability

There is no universally accepted definition of these concepts; you are not expected to memorize the definitions that follow: what matters is your understanding of these concepts, both in general and in business management.

- **Change** refers to modification or transformation over time or across places. In business management, change is usually the result of internal or external influences. For example, externally, new competitors and new trends in consumer behaviour may lead an organization to adapt its objectives and operations; internally, the arrival of a new CEO may lead to a shift in the priorities of the organization's strategic plan.

- **Creativity** refers to the process of generating new ideas and considering existing ideas from new perspectives. It includes the ability to recognize the value of ideas when developing innovative responses to problems. In business management, creativity is closely linked to innovation; for

example, it may lead to the incremental or radical improvement of a business idea, of a product or of a process, in order to be more successful or more competitive. Creativity is relevant in all parts of an organization, especially marketing and operations.

- **Ethics** refer to the moral principles and values that form the basis of how a person or an organization conducts their activities. In business management, it is important to realize that every decision may have moral implications, impacting on internal and external stakeholders and the natural environment. Ethics is expected throughout the organization, from marketing communication to operations, from recruitment of new staff to accounting practices.

- **Sustainability** refers to the ability of the present generation to meet its needs without compromising the ability of future generations to meet their own needs. Sustainable development includes conserving resources, finding more efficient ways to produce, and discovering new resources. In business management, decisions should consider the triple bottom line of people, planet and profitability, and their resulting impact, taking into account not only financial aspects, but also communities and the natural environment.

Exam guidance and strategies

Manage your time effectively: every year, students lose marks through time mismanagement. A common tendency is to spend too long on the first questions (possibly because they seem easier and more accessible) at the expense of the others. Note that the IB allows five minutes of reading time before the start of each exam; you can use this time to decide which questions you will answer, as there is usually a choice (for example: 1 question out of 2 in Section B of paper 1). For business management exams, you notionally have two minutes per mark, so you should spend at least 20 minutes on the 10 marks question of paper 1.

Read the question carefully: pay close attention to the command terms, to the way the question is formulated and what you are asked to do. You must answer the question asked, not a question that may seem similar and that you have pre-prepared and memorized.

Use business management terminology: show the examiner that you know the language of the subject – throughout your paper, and not just when you answer "definition" questions. Write about stakeholders and business strategies, make references to the business functions, show that you can accurately employ terms such as capital expenditure, non-financial motivation, marketing mix, diversification, outsourcing, production methods, economies of scale – this way, your answers will read like business management answers, not generic, common knowledge ones.

Do

- Read the instructions on the cover of your exam paper to remind you of the exam regulations, especially the number of questions you should answer in each section.
- Underline the command terms in the questions and focus on these as you work through each question.
- Write a brief plan for the longer answers in order to give them a logical structure.
- Observe the mark weighting of the sub-parts of structured questions.
- Complete the correct number of questions.
- Make sure that all your answers are legible and correctly numbered.

Don't

- Fill your answer with irrelevant content just to make it look longer. Examiners are after quality, not quantity.
- Leave the examiner to draw conclusions if you cannot decide (for example at the end of a question with the command term "recommend").
- Spend too long on your best question at the expense of others.

Key features of the book

Topic summaries focus on the main points of the sub-units. They give you basic definitions and cover all the key contents on which you may be examined.

Annotated student answers show you real answers written by previous IB candidates, which mark they achieved and why. Positive or negative feedback on student's response is given in the green and red pull-out boxes. The comments will help you understand how marks may be scored or missed.

Content link

Link to your IA

Links to your IA (internal assessment) help you connect your IA and your exam revision, as your IA is a case study where the course contents are applied.

Link to other sub-units

Content links to other sub-units connect different sub-units that you could revise together, as they offer complementary perspectives on the same topic.

QUESTION PRACTICE

An **exam paper icon** indicates that the question has been taken from a past IB paper.

>> Assessment tip

Assessment tips give advice to help you optimize your exam techniques, warning against common errors and showing how to approach particular questions and command terms.

Concept link

Concept links connect the contents of the sub-unit to the concepts of **change**, **creativity**, **ethics**, and **sustainability**.

Test yourself

Test yourself features contain questions relating to the main text, which invite students to consolidate their learning.

>> Revision tip

Revision tips give advice to help you structure your revision.

1 INTRODUCTION TO BUSINESS MANAGEMENT

You should know:

✔ What is a business?

✔ Types of business entities

✔ Business objectives

✔ Stakeholders

✔ Growth and evolution

✔ Multinational companies (MNCs)

1.1 WHAT IS A BUSINESS?

You should be able to:

✔ describe the nature of business

✔ distinguish between the four economic sectors of activity, and explain the nature of business activity in each

✔ examine the main issues around entrepreneurship

✔ analyse the challenges and opportunities for starting up a business.

This sub-unit gives you an initial framework to understand what businesses do, how they operate and how they are organized. It emphasizes the importance of "entrepreneurs" who set up new commercial ventures and are essential to business activity.

Topic summary

All businesses, from small start-ups to huge multinational conglomerates, are based on the same principles:

• They combine **resources** (human, physical and financial) with **enterprise** (entrepreneurial skills to turn a business idea into a commercial reality): those are the *inputs*.

• They produce (tangible) **goods** and/or (intangible) **services** for their customers: those are the *outputs*.

• They are organized in **four key business functions** (human resources, finance and accounts, marketing, operations) that are interdependent.

• They operate in at least one of the **four economic sectors**: primary, secondary, tertiary, quaternary; some organizations operate in several sectors. Sectoral change is possible through vertical integration; together with horizontal integration, it enables businesses to grow.

An essential element of business management is **enterprise**; this term can refer to one organization (an enterprise = a business venture) or to a skillset (also called **entrepreneurship**). **Entrepreneurs** are people who demonstrate enterprise and initiative to set up a new business. This may be for a range of reasons, such as finding a gap in the market, independence (being self-employed, as opposed to working for someone else) or personal interest and passion. Social entrepreneurs set up organizations in order to solve community-based problems, rather than to make profit for profit's sake. They are focused on their mission and the impact they want to have on society.

The process of setting up a new business differs from country to country, especially in terms of legislation, but certain features are usually present:

- There must be a basic business idea (which can be market-driven or service-driven).

- Planning is important; it may involve carrying out initial market research to ensure that the idea is commercially viable, i.e. that there is sufficient market demand (i.e. potential customers).

- Establishing legal requirements: in most countries, all new business must be registered with the local authorities.

- In many cases, the entrepreneur may need to raise funds to set up the business (**start-up costs**) and to write a comprehensive document (called a **business plan**) to attract funds and to support the launch of the new organization.

- New enterprises may fail for a range of reasons, such as unreliable suppliers or underperforming workforce, inappropriate target market, cash flow management problems, inappropriate location.

Test yourself

Can you represent visually each economic sector in the form of a drawing or with symbols? This is not an exam question, but this creative challenge can help you check that you understand and remember the differences between them.

QUESTION PRACTICE

This question is based on a previous paper 1 exam, the case study of *Utopia*, a holiday resort located on the island of Ratu, in the Pacific Islands.

With reference to *Utopia*, explain the differences between secondary sector activities and tertiary sector activities. [4]

SAMPLE STUDENT ANSWER

Secondary sector activities:

Secondary sector activities are determined as the production phase. This means that in the case of Utopia, the phase when the villas were being built. First by John and then by the local craftsmen. This had to be redone when the natural disaster in 2016 happened.

▼ The candidate shows that they know the meaning of "secondary sector" and "tertiary sector". However they did not answer the question asked: they answered "define secondary sector activities and tertiary sector activities" – they did not "explain the differences", as required by the command term of the question.

Tertiary sector activities:

Tertiary sector activities include the sale of the product to the customer. This means that, in this case the many different services, such as the boat drive and the villas are sold to the customer.

This response could have achieved 2/4 marks.

 Assessment tip

Command terms are very important – in business management, as in all other subjects. It is not enough to master the subject contents. You must follow the instructions of the command terms in order to achieve the highest marks; otherwise your answer will remain partial, even if you know the right answer. In the exam, before you start writing, make sure you closely read the question, unpacking its demands. Here, the candidate should have written about the differences between the two sectors, rather than defining one, then the other.

 Revision tip

The four business functions (human resources, finance and accounts, marketing and operations) are at the core of business management:

- They must be addressed in the business plan written by the entrepreneur or the social enterpreneur.
- They help identify the areas of internal strengths and weaknesses of a SWOT analysis.
- They correspond to the way the curriculum is structured (Unit 2: Human resource management, Unit 3: Finance and accounts, Unit 4: Marketing and Unit 5: Operations management).

Make sure you understand "the big picture" of how the course is structured, as it will help you organize your revision.

 Assessment tip

Business management is an applied subject. You must always apply your answers to the scenario given (the case study for paper 1 and paper 3, the short stimulus materials for paper 2). The only exception is definition questions such as "define the term" where you may write a 'theoretical' answer, without reference to an example.

 Content link

Link to your IA

As you work on your IA, find out how and when the organization was set up, by whom and why. Who was/were the entrepreneurs? What were their reasons and motivations? Did they write a business plan? Did they encounter particular challenges? What were the first legal requirements? Even if you do not write about these aspects in your IA, these questions can help your IA research, and your IA gives you the chance to learn more about the contents of this sub-unit in context.

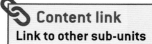

Content link

Link to other sub-units

- This sub-unit introduces unit 1 in general, so all other sub-units are closely linked to it.

- Sub-unit 3.1 is closely linked as business plans must mention the intended sources of finance of the new business (for example loan capital, the most common one).

Concept link

The concepts of **ethics** and **creativity** are closely linked to this sub-unit:

- Social enterprises have a strong sense of **ethics**: they are transparent to their stakeholders, aim to have ethical practices and are very aware of their social responsibility.

- Entrepreneurship is closely linked to **creativity**: entrepreneurs and social entrepreneurs want to try and do something new, or something different, from inventing and commercializing new products to redesigning ways of thinking and making the world a better place.

1.2 TYPES OF BUSINESS ENTITIES

This sub-unit classifies all organizations in a small number of categories, depending on their legal status.

You should be able to:

✔ distinguish between private and public sector

✔ discuss the main features of the following four types of for-profit (commercial) organizations:

  ✔ sole traders

  ✔ partnerships

  ✔ privately held companies

  ✔ publicly held companies

✔ discuss the main features of the following three types of for-profit social enterprises:

  ✔ cooperatives

  ✔ private sector companies

  ✔ public sector companies

✔ discuss the main features of one type of non-profit social enterprises: non-governmental organizations (NGOs).

Topic summary

The **public sector** refers to government-owned and government-operated organizations (for example public hospitals, the army or the police) whereas the **private sector** refers to organizations that are privately owned; they can be profit-making (to maximize dividends for their shareholders, i.e. their owners) or non-profit making (and their surplus is usually reinvested in their mission).

The four main types of for-profit (commercial) enterprises (**sole traders, partnerships** and **privately held (owned) companies** and **publicly held (owned) companies** have different legal status and are suitable for different types of businesses, according to factors such as size, ownership, liability and finance.

A **social enterprise** is a business which has a social purpose; it can be profit-making (for example a housing **cooperative**) or non-profit (for example an **NGO** which uses its **surplus** to advance the social cause it is defending).

Types of business entities, their legal status and even their names vary a lot from country to country, but there are standard features that you must know about, as well as their respective advantages and disadvantages (for example, a sole trader has total control over all important decisions, but with unlimited liability in case of faults, debts or mistakes).

>> **Revision tip**

The notion of "liability" constitutes a key difference between a sole trader and a limited company. A sole trader is responsible (i.e. liable) for all the debts of the business: this is called "unlimited liability". A limited company is called "limited" because it has "limited liability": in case of a problem (e.g. bankruptcy) the investors (shareholders) can only lose up to the value of their shares, and nothing more. They are not responsible for the other debts the company may have. In a balance sheet, the term "liabilities" refers to what the company owes to other firms, for example debts or payment to suppliers or a long-term loan that must be gradually repaid, with interest, to a bank.

>> **Revision tip**

A common misunderstanding noted by examiners is that many candidates wrongly believe that sole traders always work on their own. The word "sole" does not mean that they work alone: a sole trader may have employees.

>> **Revision tip**

There are eight types of business entities. You must be able to define each one, to explain its main features, and to compare and contrast it to other types. You also must be able to recommend the most appropriate one to a given situation; to do so, you must understand their respective advantages and disadvantages.

QUESTION PRACTICE

Outline **two** characteristics of an NGO (Non Governmental Organization). [2]

SAMPLE STUDENT ANSWER

NGOs usually have a humanitarian or social purpose, for example the Red Cross and the Red Crescent. Although they are independent from national governments, they often receive grants from governments and they cooperate with them.

▲ This answer scored well as the two characteristics are correct:
1) the social cause (social purpose),
2) the reference to funding from governments as a source of income.

This response could have achieved 2/2 marks.

>> **Assessment tip**

You may have an exam question asking you to **justify** a particular type of organization or a change in its legal status, for example a sole trader who has decided to enter into a partnership with others, or to form a private limited company. The command term "justify" means to "give valid reasons or evidence to support an answer or conclusion". In this case, you need to identify the reasons, explain them and evaluate them, with reference to their advantages and disadvantages in the context given. This is a demanding task.

Likewise, you may be asked to **recommend** a legal type to a given organization. The command term "recommend" means "present an advisable course of action with appropriate supporting evidence/reason in relation to a given situation, problem or issue" so you need to identify the reasons for your recommendation (for example, a partnership), explain these reasons and evaluate them, with reference to their advantages and disadvantages in the specific case. Your answer to such a question would therefore be quite long, as there is a lot to cover.

QUESTION PRACTICE

This question refers to an entrepreneur called Su who is setting up a social enterprise called *Afghan Sun* (AS), which is going to operate as a private limited company.

Explain the advantages for Su of forming *AS* as a private limited company.   [6]

SAMPLE STUDENT ANSWER

Response 1

▼ In this short answer, the candidate demonstrates some knowledge (about shares and limited liability) but this is not sufficiently developed: they should have explained what shares are (possibly with reference to dividends), what "limited liability" means, and why it is an advantage. Moreover, there is no reference to the case study, to Su and AS.

> A private limited is a company in which the shares are not offered for the public only for family members and friends. The shareholders of private limited companies enjoy limited liability.

This response could have achieved **2/6 marks.**

Response 2

▼ The topic of selling shares (to friends and family) is only briefly mentioned; the candidate does not explain why it is an advantage. The reference to "wider control over the shareholders" is not sufficiently clear, although the candidate seems to understand what a private limited company is.

▲ Limited liability is explained as an advantage.

▼ The causal link between easier set up and shares not on the stocks is not entirely clear.

▲ The reference to decision-making is interesting; it is linked to the topic of control mentioned before.

> Although AS is a social enterprise but Su has decided to operate as a private limited company. This could bring many advantages to her as an entrepreneur to her starting organization AS. One of the advantages is that:
>
> • because it is a private limited company, therefore the shares can only be sold to friends or family, this way she can have a wider control over the shareholders and that she has limited liability meaning in case of bankruptcy she will only lose the amount that she had invested.
>
> • Another advantage is that in comparison with the public-limited companies, a private-limited company is easier to start up because the shares shouldn't be on the stocks and therefore again decision makings are faster and easier too.

Note: Overall the candidate understands key advantages that private limited companies have (for example in terms of selling shares and limited liability). However the answer is not sufficiently contextualized, i.e. applied to the case study.

This response could have achieved **4/6 marks.**

Content link

Link to your IA

As you work on your IA, find out about the legal status of your organization: is it a sole trader, a private limited company, or maybe a public company? If it is a limited company, you could enquire about the number of shareholders and the dividends they receive. If it is a partnership, you could find out if the partners share the profits equally or not. Your IA gives you the chance to learn more about the contents of this sub-unit in context.

 Content link

Link to other sub-units

- Sub-units 1.2 and 1.3 are linked because there is often a relationship between the broad aim of the organization and its legal status (large corporations whose shares can be bought on the Stock Exchange are typically profit-making companies).

- Sub-units 1.2 and 2.2 are linked because there is often a relationship between the legal type of the organization and its structure (for example a small partnership will not be structured like a large public limited company).

Concept link

The concept of **change** is linked to the topic of types of business entities because small organizations, as they grow and expand, often change status (for example a sole trader who decides to become a private limited company, with two key benefits: the ability to raise more capital through shares and the protection offered by the limited liability).

 Revision tip

A common misunderstanding is that many candidates wrongly believe that "business owner" is the same as "business manager". Owners and managers are the same in some cases, for example for sole traders and some partners, but usually managers are employed by the company, by the shareholders (who are the real owners). The business does not belong to the managers; they work for it and receive a salary like all the other employees.

1.3 BUSINESS OBJECTIVES

You should be able to:

✔ distinguish between vision statement and mission statement, aims, objectives, strategies and tactics

✔ explain common business objectives including growth, profit, protecting shareholder value, and ethical objectives

✔ discuss the need for organizations to change strategic and tactical objectives in response to changes in internal and external environments

✔ discuss the evolving role, nature, and importance of corporate social responsibility (CSR).

This sub-unit emphasizes the importance of long-term business objectives, including ethical objectives.

Topic summary

Most organizations have a written **mission statement**, which describes what they do, or a **vision statement**, which is more forward-looking and aspirational, or both.

All businesses develop through setting and reaching **objectives**; these objectives can be **strategic** (long-term), **tactical** (short-term)

or **operational** (day-to-day). The four most common objectives are: growth objectives (for example increasing market share or volume of production), profit objectives (for example increasing net profit or increasing profit margin), protecting shareholder value (through dividends), and ethical objectives (taking other stakeholders into account, such as the local community). Objectives are usually part of a wider organizational **aim**, which is linked to the organization's vision.

Why might businesses need to change objectives and strategies?

- Because of changes in the **internal** environment, for example a new chief executive officer (CEO) who has her own ideas for the direction of the organization, or because the organization itself is changing, either radically (for example through a merger with another company) or gradually (and previous strategies written many years ago are not suitable anymore).

- Because of changes in the **external** environment, for example new legislation regarding health and safety may mean that previous practices are not legal any longer, or customers may expect the organization to follow more ethical and sustainable principles.

Two main tools (models) are used to set business objectives:

- The **SWOT analysis** framework, where the four business functions (human resources, finance and accounts, marketing, and operations) help to identify the *internal* strengths and weaknesses of an organization (whereas a STEEPLE analysis helps to identify the opportunities and threats coming from the *external* environment):

	Positive	Negative
Internal (from business functions)	Strengths	Weaknesses
External (from STEEPLE)	Opportunities	Threats

▲ Figure 1.3.1   SWOT analysis

- The **Ansoff matrix**, which considers both product and market, each time in terms of "existing" (also called "current") and "new":

		Product	
		Existing	New
Market	Existing	Market penetration	Product development
	New	Market development	Diversification

▲ Figure 1.3.2   The Ansoff matrix

SWOT analysis and the Ansoff matrix are very important models that all candidates should know and understand; however examiners always note the same common errors:

- In the Ansoff matrix, some candidates often get confused between "product development" and "market development". When they draw the matrix, some candidates forget to label the rows and columns ("Existing product", "New product" etc.) so the model is not complete.

- In the SWOT analysis, many candidates forget that the Opportunities and Threats must be external (so for example they write that "workforce going on strike" is a threat or that "using social media for marketing" is an opportunity; this is not correct).

>> Revision tip

A common misunderstanding noted by examiners is that many candidates get confused between "mission statement" and "vision statement":

- The mission statement is a description in the present tense; for example the charity *Reach Out* (the subject of a Paper 1 case study a few years ago) was set up to support the families of children with autism. It has the following vision statement: *"no child with autism will be left behind"* and the following mission statement:

  Reach Out provides online support for families of children with autism and offers them communication resources at a greatly reduced price.

  The vision statement is clearly about the future and is aspirational, whereas the mission statement describes what the organization does.

- The vision statement is a description of where the organization wants a community, or the world, to be as a result of their actions and services; for example the charity *Alzheimer's Association* (https://www.alz.org/about/strategic-plan) has the following vision statement:

  A world without Alzheimer's disease.

Make sure you understand how mission and vision statements differ, and also what is important about the messages they give to their stakeholders.

QUESTION PRACTICE

MSS is a school for girls located in Tanzania. It has a mission statement and a vision statement.

Explain, with reference to *MSS*, the purpose of the mission and vision statements. [6]

SAMPLE STUDENT ANSWER

Mission statement declares the underlying purpose of the business and states what the business is and what it does. Vision statement is basically the long-term goals and aspirations of the company.

It basically states what the business intends to achieve in the future. The main long-term goal of MSS is to achieve economies of scale by expanding their school to various cities and countries. This vision allows the staff and employees to realize what they are working towards. It also affects the turnover rate as employees who are not satisfied with the vision of the organization may leave the company. The mission statement allows the customer to understand the main purpose of the business. The mission statement affects the size of the customer base as the main

▲ The answer starts well: the candidate shows that they understand the difference between vision statement and mission statement – and they apply the two to the case study.

▼ The wording is sometimes unclear, for example when the candidate writes "the main purpose of the mission statement is to attract more students". Yes, the school wants to attract more students, but this is not the purpose of their mission statement itself: the purpose of the mission statement is to communicate what needs to be done in order to achieve the vision.

▼ Towards the end of the answer, the candidate only copies extracts from the case study, for example about the purpose of the school ("to provide high quality education…"). There is no added value and the candidate cannot get marks from just lifting sentences from the case.

purpose of the mission statement is to attract more students. The main purpose of MMS is to provide high quality education for girls from low income families.

Note: The beginning of the answer was better than the end, where the answer loses some clarity and focus.

This response could have achieved 4/6 marks.

QUESTION PRACTICE

John has two businesses on the island of Ratu in the Pacific Islands: a holiday resort called *Utopia*, composed of 24 villas, and a café called *JAC* where he sells fair trade coffee.

Explain the role of ethics in John's businesses.   [6]

SAMPLE STUDENT ANSWER

▲ Right from the start, the answer combines "theory" and "practice" i.e. the candidate shows their theoretical knowledge (of ethics in business) both in general and in the applied context of John and *Utopia*.

▲ The answer includes subject terminology all along (e.g. brand, brand image) which shows that the candidate masters all aspects of the subject well (with references to marketing, in this case).

▲ After explaining positive aspects of the role of ethics (especially about marketing), the candidate now writes about negative aspects (notably about finance).

Ethics play a role in both of John's businesses, but more so in Utopia. Ethics are actions taken based on morals and ideals. There are many ethical implications involved with Utopia. John's focus on the local community of the Pacific Islands provides employment opportunities and support for this population. His emphasis on buying ethically produced, fair trade materials (i.e. Aora Coffee) in favour of cheaper, but probably more unethical products is part of Utopia's brand. He has created a brand image of Utopia based on ethical practices and the local culture. In this way, the role of ethics for Utopia is not just part of John's personal beliefs, but is part of his marketing and Utopia's unique selling proposition. However, it can also be argued that Utopia has unethical elements, such as the fact that its presence is most likely negatively affecting the natural environment of its "beautiful location". Ethical practices are also more expensive (such as Aora coffee) and could be a contributor to Utopia's recent financial losses. JAC has less of an ethics-focused approach than Utopia, but is still based on fair trade Aora coffee rather than its cheaper and more unethical alternatives. Due to its educational activities and displays, customers can also be educated about the coffee's origins and fair trade background, which both spreads John's vision, and contributes to positive public opinion surrounding the JAC brand image.

Note: The answer is thorough and balanced. It could be even better, for example the candidate could have written more explicitly about corporate social responsibility (CSR); however what is written sufficiently fulfils the criteria for a top mark.

This response could have achieved 6/6 marks.

 Content link

Link to your IA

As you work on your IA, find out about the strategic objectives of your chosen organization. Does it have a mission statement and a vision statement? Have they changed over time? Who is responsible for setting the strategic, tactical and operational objectives? Is business **ethics** an issue for your chosen organization? You have probably prepared a SWOT analysis of your organization – but how about the Ansoff matrix: can you apply it to your organization? Your IA gives you the chance to learn more about the contents of this sub-unit in context.

Content link

Link to other sub-units

- Sub-units 1.3 and 1.5 are linked because growth is the objective of many organizations, though not all of them.

Concept link

The concepts of **ethics and change** are linked to the topic of organizational/business objectives:

- **Ethical objectives** are becoming more important for all businesses, in all organizational aspects (human resources, finance and accounts, marketing, and operations). An increasing number of businesses are becoming aware of their corporate social responsibility (CSR), and many social enterprises are built around their ethical objectives.

- Organizational objectives must be regularly reviewed to respond to **changes** in the internal and external environments; some changes can be anticipated (for example customer trends or patterns in demographics affecting the workforce), others cannot (for example a financial crisis in the national economy, a pandemic, or the arrival of a strong competitor in the market).

1.4   STAKEHOLDERS

This short sub-unit introduces a key term in business management: stakeholders. Stakeholders can be internal or external – but they are always affected by the actions of the organization.

You should be able to:

✔ identify the internal and external stakeholders of an organization

✔ explain the interests of internal and external stakeholders

✔ discuss possible areas of mutual benefit and conflict between stakeholders' interests.

Topic summary

The stakeholders are all the people who have an interest in the success of an organization because they are directly affected by its actions and performance. There is a difference between:

* **internal stakeholders**, such as employees, managers, shareholders

* **external stakeholders**, such as customers, suppliers, pressure groups or people in the local community.

A stakeholder may be an individual (for example the CEO of an organization or its founder, the entrepreneur who first set it up) or a group (for example trade unions or the government or local authorities).

Stakeholders have different **interests**; they may occasionally have very different opinions and come into **conflict** with one another. For example, the CEO of a factory may want to increase production to meet customer demand; this could lead to an increase in employment, but local environmentalists and the local authorities could be concerned by the subsequent pollution.

> **>> Assessment tip**
>
> It can sometimes be ambiguous to decide if a stakeholder is internal or external, for example business consultants are usually external but when they are employed by a company, typically on a contractual basis, they become internal, so if you have an exam question specifically about internal or external stakeholders, it is better and safer to choose straightforward examples.

QUESTION PRACTICE

Utopia is a holiday resort located on the island of Ratu in the Pacific Ocean.

With reference to *Utopia*, describe the importance of **two** external stakeholders.   [4]

SAMPLE STUDENT ANSWER

Response 1

The text states that "John deliberately resists pressure from external stakeholders to expand Utopia's capacity". External stakeholders means individuals or organizations that are not part of the business but have interests towards business activities. Government and pressure groups can be external stakeholders as they saw the potential growth of Utopia. They think expanding its capacity can attract more tourists.

▼ This short definition is correct; however the question is not "define the term external stakeholder". This initial definition is not credited: this is not what the question asked.

▲ The candidate correctly identified two external stakeholders: government and pressure groups; however their importance is not described. This is a partial answer.

This response could have achieved 2/4 marks.

>> **Assessment tip**

For questions about stakeholders, you will always be asked to refer to a specific organization from the case study or the stimulus material. Make sure that you consider the context, the scenario given: do not write about trade unions in the case of a sole trader who does not have any employees.

SAMPLE STUDENT ANSWER

Response 2

External stakeholders refer to individuals or organizations who are not part of the business but have a direct interest in its operations. In this case, the two external stakeholders can be customers and suppliers. Customers are important not only because they buy the goods and services of the business but also because they promote the business; for example, Utopia relies heavily on word of mouth for promotion which is done by the customers. Suppliers are important as they affect the price and quality of the product. For example, Utopia serves high quality coffee; however, it is expensive.

▲ The two stakeholders are identified: customers and suppliers – so at this point, the candidate has already scored 2 marks.

▲ The candidate tells us why customers are particularly important: not just as a direct source of income, but because the business relies on word of mouth promotion (a reference to the case study).

▲ The candidate tells us why suppliers are particularly important for the *Utopia* brand, with a financial dimension too (they supply ethically produced fair trade Aora coffee; however it is expensive (reference to the case study)). The answer is clear and thorough overall.

This response could have achieved 4/4 marks.

This diagram shows the comparative closeness of stakeholders to decision-making:

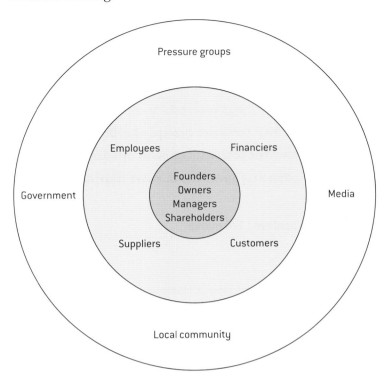

▲ **Figure 1.4.1** The comparative closeness of stakeholders to decision-making

 Content link

Link to your IA

As you work on your IA, identify the main internal and external stakeholders of your organization. Can you also identify some possible areas of conflict between some stakeholders? You could decide to explore this in your IA, especially as criterion B refers to a range of perspectives (you can read more about this in the section about the IA on pages 110–114).

 Content link

Link to other sub-units

- Sub-units 1.4 and 1.5 are linked because a company's growth and evolution will affect many stakeholders, both internally (such as shareholders who may receive more dividends) and externally (such as the government through more taxes).

- Sub-units 1.4 and 2.7 (HL only) are linked because the conflicts between employers and employees, at the core of industrial relations, are conflicts between stakeholders who have different concerns and priorities.

- Sub-units 1.4 and 5.7 (HL only) are linked because an essential aspect of crisis management is good, fast, transparent and honest communication with stakeholders.

Concept link

The concept of **ethics** is linked to the topic of stakeholders because some stakeholders may place ethics very high on their list of criteria when choosing an employer or a supplier. It is often said that millennials tend to consider issues of **ethics**, **sustainability** and impact on the environment much more seriously than previous generations.

1.5 GROWTH AND EVOLUTION

You should be able to:

✔ explain internal and external "economies of scale" and "diseconomies of scale"

✔ evaluate the reasons why businesses may decide to grow or to stay small

✔ distinguish between internal growth and external growth

✔ discuss the following five methods of external growth:

  ✔ mergers and acquisitions (M&As)

  ✔ takeovers

  ✔ joint ventures

  ✔ strategic alliances

  ✔ franchising.

This sub-unit introduces important terms (such as "economies of scale") and processes (such as "external growth") which help understand why and how businesses may change and grow (e.g. through "joint ventures" or "franchises").

Topic summary

Economies of scale are the reduction in average unit cost as a business increases in size. The opposite is **diseconomies of scale**: an increase in average unit cost as the business increases in size. Economies of scale are desirable; they may be due to internal factors (such as purchasing in bulk and getting discounts from suppliers) or external factors (such as concentration of customers in one area); likewise, diseconomies of scale may be due to internal factors (such as "over-specialized" managers) or external factors (such as a shortage of skilled workers meaning that the business may have to pay them higher wages to retain them).

Not all businesses want to expand. Large organizations have many advantages (including economies of scale, higher status and increased market share); however small organizations have many advantages too (such as greater focus on customers and competitive advantage in small niche markets).

Internal (organic) growth refers to the slow growth of a business occurring "from within", i.e. out of its existing operations; risks are limited, and expansion is often self-financed using retained profits. Example of internal growth: a successful hotel that purchases its neighbouring buiding to expand, or a large school that decides to offer the IBDP on top of its existing provision. **External (fast-track) growth** is quicker but riskier; it involves some arrangements to work with another existing business. The five main methods of external growth are:

- **Mergers and acquisitions (M&As),** when the businesses are completely integrated.

- When the acquisition is unwanted by the company being acquired, the term used is **takeover** or **hostile takeover**.

- **Joint venture,** the creation of a separate business entity by the two "parent" companies, for a finite period of time; the two companies still exist separately (and are "partners" in the joint venture).

- **Strategic alliances**, agreements by two (or more) companies to work together for mutual benefit; unlike a joint venture, no new business is created.

- **Franchising**, a process whereby an original business (the franchisor) sells to another business (the franchisee) the right to use its business model, brand and products. Franchises are very common in most countries, from McDonalds to The Body Shop. Franchises have many advantages for the franchisor (for example no risk, but financial gains) and for the franchisee (as for example the product already exists and is usually well-known); however there are many disadvantages too (for example the franchisee has no control over what to sell, and the franchisor could see its image suffer if the franchise fails).

QUESTION PRACTICE

TM is a chain of supermarkets which has historically used internal growth to develop, as its attempts at external growth through franchising were unsuccessful.

Explain the advantages for *TM* of internal growth rather than external growth. **[6]**

SAMPLE STUDENT ANSWER

Response 1

▼ The candidate seems to confuse "internal/external growth" and "internal/external source of finance". Little may be credited in this answer, except the idea that "internal" means "from inside the company".

> Internal growth means it comes from inside the company with their own money. They open more stores without borrowing money from external sources like banks as they have to repay with interest.

This response could have achieved 1/6 marks.

Response 2

▼ The candidate has some correct knowledge about the topic of internal growth. The answer however is only theoretical. The candidate seems to write only what they have memorized; the answer here reads like a summary from a textbook. The section of the answer about "disadvantages" is not relevant. There is no application to the business (*TM*). The candidate is not using relevant information from the case study (such as the unsuccessful franchising and the system of rigid control that may be difficult to implement with strategies of external growth).

> Internal growth means expansion from within the business, for example by product development, market development, or increasing the number of business units and their location.
>
> The advantages of internal growth are: less risk than external growth, builds on the company's strength (for example its brand name), more control.
>
> The disadvantages of internal growth are: slow growth, hard to build a market if not already a market leader, may miss opportunities to collaborate with other companies (synergies).

This response could have achieved 2/6 marks.

Response 3

Internal growth has many advantages for TM:

Internal growth is easy for TM because their brand name is famous: when they open a new supermarket, they will get customers because everybody knows them, like Walmart.

They can keep the same managers and ask them to open the new supermarkets (like a team of professional TM supermarket openers).

They don't have to worry about working with other businesses or creating alliances and having disagreements and culture clash.

Staff know they can get promotion at work or move from one supermarket to the other, if they want to work in a different town, or at a different post.

They can keep control of what they sell and how, with their own brand and their own methods, so franchising could really work for them, but it says that it didn't).

▲ This is a good answer. The points made are not always very well written but this is not a problem: the candidate, in their own words, shows that they fully understand the advantages of internal growth for *TM*. For a higher mark, the last point could be clearer, about franchising, as franchising is external.

This response could have achieved 5/6 marks.

Content link
Link to other sub-units

- Sub-units 1.5 and 2.1 are linked because growth involves workforce planning, so the company will need an HR strategy (either to employ more employees, or to lay off some employees in the case of a merger where some posts may become redundant).

- Sub-units 1.5 and 3.2 are linked because growth needs to be funded (either internally, usually through retained profit, or externally, for example through share capital or loan capital).

- Sub-units 1.5 and 4.5 are linked because growth and evolution have an impact on the company's marketing mix (especially if the company's products are at different stages of their lifecycles, needing different pricing strategies, different marketing approaches and different channels of distribution).

- Sub-units 1.5 and 5.8 (HL only) are linked because research and development are important factors that lead the growth and evaluation of a company.

Content link
Link to your IA

Depending on the size and type of the organization you study, topics such as joint venture and franchising may not be relevant for you, but other aspects from this sub-unit are relevant to all organizations. For your chosen organization, what would represent "economies of scale" and "diseconomies of scale"? Why? And how could your organization grow (a) internally, and (b) externally? With such questions, your IA gives you the chance to learn more about the contents of this sub-unit in context.

Concept link

The concept of **change** is closely linked to the topic of growth and evolution because growth and evaluation are processes of change, usually about an increase in size and scope (though some sole traders and small companies purposefully decide to remain small).

1.6   MULTINATIONAL COMPANIES (MNCs)

This short sub-unit introduces a key term of the world of contemporary business: globalization. In the context of globalization, it focuses on the impact of MNCs on their host countries.

You should be able to:

✔ define the term globalization

✔ explain the growth of MNCs

✔ discuss the impact of MNCs on the host countries.

Topic summary

Globalization refers to the increasing flow of ideas, financial transactions, goods and services around the world.

A wide range of international forces (such as the increasing social, cultural, technological and economic integration) influence business organizations – and, in turn, business organizations shape these forces, contributing to the greater integration and understanding of countries and cultures. All businesses and consumers are influenced by global forces, directly or indirectly.

In the context of globalization, **multinational companies (MNCs)** that operate in more than one country have grown rapidly, thanks to improved communications, fewer trade barriers and market deregulation. MNCs have both positive and negative impacts on the countries where they operate: positive impacts such as economic growth (through employment opportunities) and possibly infrastructure projects, but also negative impacts such as profits being sent back to headquarters abroad and loss of market share for local businesses.

🔗 Content link

Link to your IA

For your IA, you could decide to study a concept in the context of a MNC (such as Starbucks, Chanel or the Mahindra Group). In this case, it could be very helpful for you to explore how this company first developed in its home country (for example: Starbucks in the USA, Chanel in France, and the Mahindra Group in India) and how it gradually expanded into other countries. Your IA gives you the chance to learn more about the contents of this sub-unit in context.

≫ Assessment tip

For Paper 1, Paper 2 or Paper 3, if your case study is about an MNC, think about the external stakeholders that may be affected by its activities:

1. Why are consumers particularly attracted? Is it because of the well-known global brand?

2. Are suppliers local? Do local producers benefit from the presence of the MNC?

3. Does the MNC pay taxes locally? Does it benefit the local community and the local economy, or are all profits sent back to the home country of the MNC?

Content link

Link to other sub-units

This sub-unit is particularly linked to:

- Sub-unit 1.5, as expanding internationally can be done through M&As, takeovers, joint ventures, strategic alliances, and franchising.

- Sub-unit 3.2, as internal or external sources of finance are essential to grow internationally.

- Sub-unit 4.6 (HL only), as international marketing represents both opportunities and risks for MNCs, who must balance globalization and the specificities of national markets ('think globally, act locally').

Concept link

The three concepts of change, ethics, and sustainability are relevant for MNCs:

- **Change**, because many MNCs decide to adapt their operations and practices to the countries where they operate (for example, McDonald's offers different menus and products in different countries, such as more vegetarian options in India and croissants in France);

- **Ethics**, because some MNCs have been accused of working with suppliers, partners or contractors that had unethical practices, especially in developing countries, for example in 'sweatshops' employing children;

- **Sustainability**, because some aspects of globalization are unsustainable, such as international trade, logistics and transport, to the detriment of shorter distribution channels and local development.

≫ Revision tip

Most terms in business management may be defined in several ways, using synonymous expressions; for example you could define **franchise** as a contract or an agreement or a relationship between two businesses or two organizations. A small number of terms, however, have a specific technical definition that you must memorize by heart, such as **economies of scale**, the reduction in average unit cost as a business increases in size.

2 HUMAN RESOURCE MANAGEMENT

You should know:

✔ Role and importance of human resource management

✔ Organizational structure

✔ Leadership and management

✔ Motivation and demotivation

✔ Organizational (corporate) culture (HL only)

✔ Communication

✔ Industrial/employee relations (HL only)

2.1 INTRODUCTION TO HUMAN RESOURCE MANAGEMENT

This sub-unit introduces the topic of human resources (HR), one of the four essential business functions. It emphasizes the factors that influence human resource planning and the concept of **change** in HR.

You should be able to:

✔ explain the role of human resource management

✔ explain the main internal and external factors that influence human resource planning

✔ explain reasons for resistance to change in the workplace

✔ discuss human resource strategies for reducing the impact of change and resistance to change in organizations.

Topic summary

Human resource (HR) management includes workforce planning, specifying job responsibilities, recruiting staff, and setting their financial and non-financial rewards. It is essential for all organizations, irrespective of their size, of their legal status and of their sector of activity.

Numerous factors can influence an organization's HR plan:

*   External factors such as demographic change, change in labour mobility and new communication technologies.

*   Internal factors such as changes in business organization (for example: restructure, streamlining) or changes in business strategy (for example: internal or external growth).

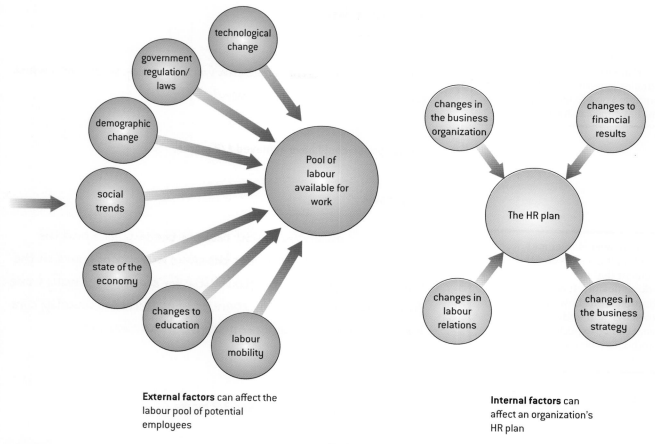

External factors can affect the labour pool of potential employees

Internal factors can affect an organization's HR plan

▲ Figure 2.1.1 External and internal factors influencing an HR plan

The following five aspects are particularly important:

- **demographic changes**, including retirement age, gender balance, birth rates, longevity etc,

- **changes in labour mobility**, domestically (within the same country) or internationally,

- immigration, temporarily or permanently,

- the **increase in flexitime**, flexible work schedules allowing workers to adjust their starting and finishing times, giving them the flexibility to meet other demands (such as childcare requirements),

- the development of a "**gig economy**" where many positions are temporary and organizations hire independent workers for short-term commitments.

Employers and employees are all affected by changes in work patterns, practices and preferences, such as teleworking and job sharing. Sometimes employees welcome changes in the workplace, but sometimes they are resistant, for a range of reasons, such as fear and discomfort, insufficient reward, lack of skills, mistrust, poor communication, poor timing or prior experience of change management. Organizations can adopt a range of human resource strategies to reduce the negative impacts of change and resistance to change, for example developing a vision for the change process and the desired outcomes, communicating it clearly to all employees and training them before the changes are implemented.

QUESTION PRACTICE

Define the term *flexitime*. [2]

SAMPLE STUDENT ANSWER

Response 1

▼ This answer has some value but it remains superficial, with a rather "common knowledge" approach of what flexitime can mean.

Flexitime means that people can work flexibly, when they want, for example evenings or weekends.

This response could have achieved 1/2 marks.

Response 2

▲ This answer is clear and thorough; it goes beyond the mere statement that flexitime means working flexibly. It is a technical definition with shows very good knowledge and understanding – what can be expected from a candidate who has studied the topic!

Flexitime is an arrangement between the employee and the employer. The employee works the same number of hours in the week, but they have some flexibility; for example she may work from 8am to 4pm or from 10am to 6pm. There are usually core hours, but the starting time and finishing time are more flexible.

This response could have achieved 2/2 marks.

▶▶ Assessment tip

For Paper 1 and Paper 2, you will have some "define" questions. Make sure you sufficiently develop your ideas: do not opt for a mimimal answer (as short as possible). Write more than one sentence! These questions are always worth 2 marks. There is no minimum of words, but if your answer is too short, you will score only 1 mark. You have time to write more text and to show the examiner that you know the meaning of the term you are asked to define.

Content link
Link to your IA

Once you have chosen your organization for your IA, you should do some background research about human resources in that organization, even if you do not plan to focus on an HR topic. HR is a broad topic: you could research how many people are employed, who they are (in terms of demographics: age, gender, level of education etc) and what type of contract they have (full-time, part-time). This can help you better understand the organization, some of its strengths but also some of its weaknesses. Your IA gives you the chance to learn more about the contents of this sub-unit in context.

Content link

Link to other sub-units

This sub-unit introduces Unit 2 in general, so it is relevant for all sub-units about HR. It is also linked to sub-unit 1.3 about business objectives, as organizational decisions to grow have direct impacts on HR planning and recruitment.

Concept link

This sub-unit is particularly linked to the concept of **change**, as HR management and workforce planning are all about anticipating change and adapting to change: external changes in the labour pool available for work and internal changes in the organization itself.

2.2   ORGANIZATIONAL STRUCTURE SOME HL ONLY

You should be able to:

✔ construct and interpret different types of organizational charts

✔ distinguish between key terms about organizational structure

✔ evaluate how changes in organizational structures may be appropriate

✔ evaluate changes in organizational structures (for example, project-based organization, Charles Handy's "Shamrock Organization") (HL only).

This sub-unit focuses on the way organizations are structured, showing the relationships between the employees in different parts of the hierarchy.

Topic summary

An **organizational chart** is a diagram that shows the HR structure of an organization, outlining the formal roles, responsibilities and reporting lines.

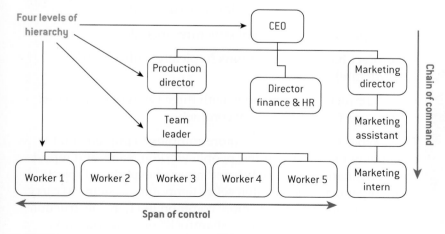

▲ **Figure 2.2.1** Example of an organizational chart

▼ Table 2.2.1 Key terms to help describe the structure of an organization

Levels of hierarchy	The number of levels of responsibility and seniority in an organization, from the most "senior" to the most "junior".
Chain of command	The formal route through which decisions travel downward.
Span of control	Number of employees reporting to a given line manager.
Delegation	When a manager gives authority for a particular decision to someone else, yet still holds responsibility for the outcome.
Centralization	Decisions are made by a small group in a senior position.
Decentralization	Decisions are made by managers throughout the organization (though senior managers retain control of key strategic decisions).
Bureaucracy	Rules and procedures within an organization.
De-layering	Removing layers of (middle) managers, reducing the levels of hierarchy.
Matrix structure	Structure combining organization by function (design, operations, finance, marketing, etc) and organization by project.

Organizational structures can be flat (horizontal) or tall (vertical):

- **Taller organizational structures** are characterized by many levels of hierarchy, narrow spans of control, centralized decision-making, longer chains of command and limited delegation.

- **Flatter organizational structures** are characterized by fewer levels of hierarchy, wider spans of control, decentralized decision-making, shorter chains of command and increased delegation.

Departments are often organized by **function** (such as "Marketing" and "Finance"), though in some MNCs it may be more suitable to organize by **region** (by market) or by **product** (or families of product).

There is not one "correct" form of structure: as organizations grow, the senior managers may decide to modify the structure and adopt a more appropriate one.

Changes in organizational structure may be due to internal or external factors, for example the need to hire more staff, including more managers, or the need to reconsider the entire structure after a merger.

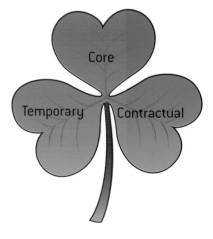

▲ Figure 2.2.2 The shamrock model

HL Changes in other organizational structures

Other types of organizational structures include:

- **project-based organizations** (typically with a **matrix** structure)

- **"shamrock"** organizations with three types of employees: (1) core, (2) temporary, (3) contractual.

Those types of structures are more complex to implement, for example in matrix structures, people work in teams and report to several managers with different areas of expertise. Project-based organizations are often set as temporary systems to carry out specific projects; this is more common in IT, in construction and in some NGOs. The term "shamrock" organization was coined by HR expert Charles Handy, using the metaphor of a shamrock plant with its three leaves.

Make sure you pay close attention to the **command term** at the start of each question. The expectations about the approach, contents and even length of your answer are different — and examiners pay very close attention to this. The following table gives you examples on the topic of **change** from a tall to a flatter structure.

Command term	IB definition	Example of question	Example of good answer
State	"Give a specific name, value or other brief answer without explanation or calculation."	**State** one advantage of changing the organization of company X from a tall to a flatter structure. [1 mark]	Fewer levels of hierarchy in company X.
Describe	"Give a detailed account."	**Describe** one advantage of changing the organization of company X from a tall to a flatter structure. [2 marks]	If company X adopts a flatter structure, there will be fewer levels of hierarchy from the top of the organization to the bottom: the pyramidal structure of the organizational chart will include fewer levels.
Explain	"Give a detailed account including reasons or causes."	**Explain** one advantage of changing the organization of company X from a tall to a flatter structure. [2 marks]	Adopting a flatter structure would have the following advantage: fewer levels of hierarchy make it easier and faster for communication to flow down the chain of command. This has been a source of problems in the past, with some middle managers complaining about this, so it would be beneficial for company X, for communication within the company and for middle managers' job satisfaction.
Analyse	"Break down in order to bring out the essential elements or structure."	**Analyse** one advantage of changing the organization of company X from a tall to a flatter structure. [3 marks]	Adopting a flatter structure means that company X would have fewer levels of hierarchy, which leads to a shorter chain of command and decentralized decision-making. As a result, many middle managers will be happy with this advantage, as they have complained about problems of communication at work; this is why the new CEO (chief executive officer) says that with a flatter structure and fewer levels of hierarchy, the atmosphere and work conditions will be better.

Concept link

The concept of **change** is linked to the topic of organizational structure. The structure of all organizations changes over time; even today's largest MNCs started with a small number of employees. These changes can be gradual, with the slow addition of more employees and more levels of hierarchy, or more sudden, when for example two companies merge, which can result in a major restructuring.

Content link
Link to your IA

Even if your IA is not specifically about human resources, you can apply the contents of this sub-unit to your chosen organization. What does its organizational chart look like? Is the structure tall or flat? How many levels of hierarchy are there? Has there been any **change** to the structure recently? Your IA gives you the chance to learn more about the contents of this sub-unit in context.

Content link
Link to other sub-units

- Sub-unit 2.3 about leadership and management is closely linked to this sub-unit about organizational structure because a manager's span of control and position in the organizational hierarchy will influence their approach, style, decisions and actions.

- Sub-unit 2.5 (HL only) about organizational culture is closely linked to this sub-unit too because the structure and the culture of an organization mutually influence each other.

2.3   LEADERSHIP AND MANAGEMENT   SOME HL ONLY

This sub-unit focuses on the differences between management and leadership, including the range of leadership styles and the factors that may influence them.

You should be able to:

✔ distinguish between management and leadership

✔ explain the difference between scientific and intuitive thinking and management (HL only)

✔ discuss the following five leadership styles: autocratic, paternalistic, democratic, laissez-faire and situational.

Topic summary

Management and leadership are closely linked. Managers can be leaders, and vice versa, but the two are different. One usually distinguishes between "**leader**" and "**manager**".

- The idea of "manager" and "management" is more about planning and organizing, setting and achieving goals by controlling situations. Managers are said to be "task-orientated".

- The idea of "leader" and "leadership" is more about inspiring and motivating staff, and about having a strategic vision for the organization. Leaders are said to be "relationship-orientated".

HL   Some managers prefer more rationale approaches based on evidence and quantitative data (known as "scientific thinking") whereas others prefer to follow their intuition and qualitative impressions.

There are numerous leadership styles, including the following five:

- **Autocratic** style, which emphasizes authority and control.

- **Paternalistic**, which places authority in a caring, family-like context.

- **Democratic**, which involves employees in the decision-making process.

- **Laissez-faire**, which gives employees more freedom and scope.

- **Situational**, which stresses the need to adapt to the situation, the decision and the context.

These five styles are not exclusive: they may overlap, for example a paternalistic leader often displays features of the autocratic leadership style. They all have advantages and disadvantages; some are more appropriate than others in given situations.

Leadership styles and management styles are influenced by many factors, such as the personality of the leader/manager, their values, the workers, their motivation, the work environment, as well as aspects of ethics and culture.

>> **Assessment tip**

Candidates usually understand management and leadership styles quite well, but their answers are sometimes too theoretical, i.e. not sufficiently applied to the case study or to the stimulus materials. Remember, our subject is applied: the examiner wants to assess your ability to apply "theory" (your knowledge of leadership styles, with the proper terminology and the correct ideas) to "practice" (the examples themselves). If your answer is too theoretical, you will not be able to reach top marks.

Further common mistakes in candidates' answers are comments that "autocratic leadership is bad" and "democratic leadership is good". The analysis and evaluation should be related to the situation and its variables.

QUESTION PRACTICE

This question refers to the case study of John Ariki, an entrepreneur who has recently founded two businesses: a resort called *Utopia* and a café called *JAC*. John manages them both.

With reference to John, explain the key functions of management. [6]

SAMPLE STUDENT ANSWER

Response 1

Managers are people who are higher in the hierarchy and rank after the M.D. or owners. Managers are expected to:

be good planners

be good decision makers

be good organizers

control the business subordinates

supervise

run and motivate their subordinates.

▲ The answer starts well: the candidate shows some theoretical knowledge of the key functions of management, with the right terminology: decision-making, planning, control, supervision, motivating workers.

▼ The answer is not applied to the organization, nor to John (even though the question started with the words "With reference to John"). The answer is short and solely theoretical; moreover, the examiner cannot be sure that the candidate really knows what "decision-making" and "motivation" mean.

This response could have achieved 2/6 marks.

Response 2

One key function of management is organizing resources and maintaining production of high-quality products or services. John, as a manager of Utopia, has been organizing natural ingredients for meals from neighbouring islands and coffee from Aora. Also, by doing so, John has been able to provide both high quality and fresh food and coffee to its customers.

▲ Right from the first paragraph, the candidate applies their answer to John, explaining what the first abstract idea ("organizing resources and maintaining production") means in the context of John's restaurant.

▲ In the second paragraph, the candidate again refers to both "theory" and "practice", using correct subject terminology (about setting objectives and paternalistic leadership style). For an even higher mark, the examiner would expect a more developed answer, for example also mentioning control or coordination.

Another key function of management is setting objectives and motivating employees to reach these objectives. John has set clear visions for both JAC and Utopia and setting clear objectives or visions not only gives direction to employees but also motivates them to work towards these visions. Also by adopting a paternalistic leadership style, John is able to discuss important decisions with his employees which will eventually give his employees motivation.

This response could have achieved 5/6 marks.

≫ Revision tip

The name of our DP subject is "Business management" so you may need to show that you know what you are studying, what our DP subject is all about. All aspects of the syllabus, from marketing to finance, from HR to operations, ultimately aim at developing your understanding of how business organizations are managed. These principles apply to profit-making ventures ("businesses" strictly speaking) but also to non-commercial organizations, in the voluntary or public sector. In all these contexts, management is about planning, organizing, allocating resources, coordinating and controlling – and you should be able to write about this. As part of your preparation, you could:

- apply the course contents to a non-profit making organization; for example, identify its "market", its "customers" and its "competitors"

- compare profit-making and non-profit-making organizations; for example, examine if marketing models may be applied in the same way

- read about famous leaders and managers of different types of organizations; explain why they have the same features and characteristics, no matter what the organization is.

QUESTION PRACTICE

This question refers to the case study of Suchenlin and the two organizations she has founded, a travel agency called High-end Holidays (*HH*) and a social enterprise called Afghan Sun (*AS*). Su has appointed several managers to help her run these two organizations.

With reference to Su and her managers at *HH* and *AS*, explain the differences between leadership and management. [6]

SAMPLE STUDENT ANSWER

Response 1

Leadership and management go hand-in-hand, both play a vital role within a business. Leadership tends to take the hands off approach as opposed to management, where they come face-to-face with the shortcomings and progression of the company. Leadership has an indirect role inside of the company while still remaining a key part to the success of the company. Management directly immerses themselves into the company. Management has a workload not only focusing on problems inside of the business but outside of the business as well. Regular communication takes place between management and leadership. New comings have to be reported to leadership; they have a close relationship.

▲ The candidate contrasts leadership and management, which shows some subject knowledge.

▼ The points made are valid (although rather abstract at times) but they are only theoretical, although the question started with the words "With reference to Su and her managers". The candidate unfortunately ignored that part of the question.

This response could have achieved 3/6 marks.

Response 2

One difference between leadership and management is that while leaders focus on the long-term plans of a business, managers handle the short- to medium-term issues that a business is facing. It is known that Su is not taking a part in the day to day running of HH and she has an input into the strategic decision making while her managers make day to day and tactical decisions.

▲ The first paragraph already shows that the candidate has understood the task well: contrasting leadership and management, with reference to Su and her managers. The first paragraph is about a first difference, well applied.

Another difference is that leadership has a more emotional quality when it comes to inspiring workers towards a common goal while managers' responsibility is to direct subordinates. While Su "provides the inspiration for HH" and "the managers are inspired by Su", the managers direct staff with a more professional approach. With the ability to motivate and inspire others, Su, as a leader, helps workers and managers to understand her mission and get together for a common goal. The managers, however, are more task-oriented.

▲ The second paragraph is about a second difference. The candidate quotes the case study, which is a good technique to substantiate their ideas. It is good to see that all through the answer, the candidate uses subject terminology, for example here using "task-oriented".

Another difference between leaders and managers is that while leaders are not afraid to take risks and welcome change, managers try to avert risks and apply the policies of the business they are working for. Su, as a leader, takes the risk of investing 200,000 into a new business when she already has enough money. The managers, however, try to avert risks by coordinating and taking tactical decisions.

▲ Third paragraph, third difference – always with a balance of "theory" and "practice". The candidate also shows that they understand the story of the case study very well.

▲ Although the question is not explicitly about leadership styles, the candidate harnesses knowledge of leadership styles very well in their answer, showing the examiner that they have mastered sub-unit 2.3. The answer is clear and thorough.

As a laissez-faire leader, Su also empowers her managers in order to motivate them and have autonomy. That is why able leadership is also concerned with motivating workers with a more people-oriented approach while managers mostly focus on their tasks such as the research they've conducted.

This response could have achieved 6/6 marks.

≫ Assessment tip

When you write long answers, it is good practice to set paragraphs. A paragraph is a coherent unit of meaning; with paragraphs, the layout of your answer shows your ability to structure your thoughts. In this last example, the candidate wrote four separate paragraphs, each corresponding to one of the differences between leadership and management. Not only is it more reader-friendly for the examiner, but it also shows the ability to organize ideas in a logical way, as opposed to writing one simple block of text with many ideas but no clear structure.

Test yourself

Explain how a good leader can also be a good manager, and how a good leader could also be a bad manager.

≫ Revision tip

As you revise the course contents, it can be useful to work with pairs of opposite terms that you can contrast, for example "leadership versus management" or "democratic versus autocratic". The reality of business management in general, and of human resources in particular, is however more nuanced than this. In your exam answers, make sure that you can also demonstrate your critical thinking skills, especially to go beyond simple oppositions. For example, you could explain how the same person can be both a leader and a manager, or how someone can adapt their leadership style according to the situation, sometimes more democratic and sometimes more autocratic.

⌕ Content link
Link to other sub-units

- Sub-unit 2.2 examines organizational structure; this is closely linked to this sub-unit, as leadership and management style should fit the structure of the organization. For example, an autocratic leadership style would be more appropriate for a tall, centralized, bureaucratic organization than for a flat, decentralized organization.

- Sub-unit 2.4 explores the topic of motivation; this is closely linked to this sub-unit, as managers and leaders must find ways to motivate their employees.

- Sub-unit 2.7 (HL only) examines the relations between employees and employers, especially in cases of conflict; this is closely linked to this sub-unit, as many conflicts are due to management and leadership styles.

Concept link

The concepts of **ethics** and **change** are linked to the topic of leadership and management:

- **Ethics** plays an increasing role in leadership and management: leaders and managers are becoming more aware of the ethical dimensions of their actions and decisions. For example, feminism has helped to raise awareness of misogynistic behaviour towards women in the workplace that is not ethically acceptable.

- Leaders and managers may need to **change** and adapt their style according to **changes** in the internal and external environment of the organization. For example, a leader who had a laissez-faire approach may need to become more autocratic if employees are underperforming and the organization's survival is at stake.

2.4 MOTIVATION AND DEMOTIVATION SOME HL ONLY

You should be able to:

✔ discuss the motivation theories from Taylor, Maslow and Herzberg

✔ distinguish between the seven types of financial rewards

✔ distinguish between the six types of non-financial rewards

✔ distinguish between the three forms of training

and for HL only:

✔ discuss the motivation theories from McClelland, Deci and Ryan and the equity and expectancy theory (HL only)

✔ calculate and interpret labour turnover (HL only)

✔ compare and contrast the main methods of internal and external recruitment (HL only)

✔ explain the following types of appraisal: formative, summative, 360-degree feedback and self-appraisal (HL only).

This sub-unit presents key ideas from influential motivation theorists and explains how, in practice, employees can be trained, motivated and rewarded, financially and non-financially. At HL, other theories and other topics are explored, such as recruitment and appraisal.

Topic summary

Motivation theories

Several **motivation theories** can help business managers understand the psychology behind workers' motivation (and demotivation):

- **Taylor**'s time and motion studies about efficiency and the standardization of working practices.

- **Maslow**'s pyramidal hierarchy of human needs (the more needs an employer can satisfy, the more motivated the employees will be).

- **Herzberg**'s basic "hygiene needs" (that must be satisfied) vs "true motivators".

Financial and non-financial rewards

There are seven types of **financial rewards**:

1. **Salary** (usually paid monthly).

2. **Wages: time rates** (possibly with overtime rates of pay) or **piece rates**.

3. **Commission** (for example a flat fee or percentage for each item sold).

4. **Profit-related pay**.

5. **PRP: Performance-related pay** (usually a bonus).

6. **Employee share ownership schemes** (payment in shares of the business, or savings plan).

7. **Fringe payments (perks)** sometimes linked to the nature of business.

There are six types of **non-financial rewards**:

1. **Job enrichment** (making the job more meaningful and rewarding).

2. **Job rotation** (also common as a form of training).

3. **Job enlargement** (which can include job enrichment and job rotation).

4. **Empowerment** (giving employees control over how to do their job).

5. **Purpose** (the opportunity to make a difference, socially or environmentally).

6. **Teamwork** (working with colleagues to achieve a common goal).

Financial and non-financial rewards may affect job satisfaction, motivation and productivity in different cultures; all financial and non-financial rewards have different degrees of effectiveness in different countries and cultures. Some workers are mostly interested in making (more) money, whereas others may respond more to non-financial rewards. Managers must consider which rewards, or combination of rewards, are more suitable, depending upon the context.

Training

Training is essential to ensure that employees receive appropriate professional development. There are different types of training, including: **induction** (at the beginning), **on the job** (through mentoring or shadowing) and **off the job** (external training).

Test yourself

Explain the main advantages and disadvantages of all the financial and non-financial rewards.

›› Assessment tip

How long should your answers be?

In business management, there is no specification about word count in exam answers. You should use three factors to help you estimate how long your answers should be, i.e. how much you should write to achieve a high mark:

1. **How many marks are allocated to the question?** For a question worth only 2 marks, you can answer in a few sentences, one paragraph at most.

2. **How much time are you expected to spend on the question?** In business management, the allocation is approximately 2 minutes per mark, so for a question worth 2 marks, you are only expected to spend 4–5 minutes. In fact, as these questions tend to be straightforward, you are likely to spend much less, thereby saving time for the longest, more demanding questions (worth 10 marks and 20 marks).

3. **What is the command term?** A straightforward command term such as "state" asks for a short answer (a few words may be enough) whereas an evaluative command term such as "discuss" implies a much longer answer with balanced arguments.

Examples:

Using Herzberg's motivation theory, explain one reason for the recent issue at TH with punctuality and absenteeism. [2 marks]	This question is only worth 2 marks, so keep your question short: a couple of sentences are enough. You do not need to write everything you remember about Herzberg's two-factor theory, such as the difference between what he calls "hygiene needs" versus "true motivators". Go to the point: the examiner expects a short answer combining "theory" (with a reference to Herzberg's ideas) and "practice" (the application to the case study: punctuality at TH in this case).
Apply Deci and Ryan's self-determination theory to the programmers at Gen Y. [6 marks]	This question is worth 6 marks, so your answer should be long and thorough; the examiner can expect you to spend at least 10 minutes answering this question, so you must show: • that you know and understand Deci and Ryan's theory • that you can apply the three concepts from their theory (competence, relatedness, autonomy) to the case study. Your answer is likely to be structured in three paragraphs, with each paragraph linking one of the three concepts to the case study (the programmers at Gen Y).

›› Assessment tip

Do not spend too much time on questions worth only 2 marks (even if you have a lot to write) and make sure you sufficiently develop your longer answers.

Sometimes, the question will ask you specifically which motivation theories to use, such as Herzberg or Deci and Ryan in these examples – but sometimes you are free to choose yourself.

HL ## Other motivation theories

Other motivation theories include:

- **McClelland's acquired needs theory**, about the fact that employees have three needs: achievement, affiliation, and power. According to McClelland, these three needs influence employees' motivation.

- **Deci and Ryan's self-determination theory**: according to them, there are two types of motivation: autonomous motivation (when a person freely chooses what do) and controlled motivation (when a person either seeks a reward or wants to avoid punishment). The three needs Deci and Ryan identified are competence, relatedness and autonomy.

- **Equity and expectancy theory**: formulated by Adams, this theory is based on the notions of inputs, outputs and equity. Employees are motivated when they feel that there is a balance between their inputs into the business (their work) and their outputs from it (the rewards they get).

HL ## Appraisal

Employers need to know about employees' levels of motivation and demotivation – and appraisal methods help them do this, whilst also evaluating employee performance. The four main methods of appraisal are:

- **Formative appraisal**: ongoing, continuous, intended to improve employees' performance.

- **Summative appraisal**: at the end of the training or at a fixed time during a year, more formal and documented, meant to measure employees' performance.

- **360-degree appraisal**, when an employee receives input from all categories of people (line manager, but also colleagues and possibly customers or subordinates.)

- **Self-appraisal**, when an employee evaluates their own performance.

HL ## Labour turnover

Levels of motivation and demotivation also help understand why employees may decide to leave their workplace; it is then possible to calculate labour turnover.

Labour turnover refers to the movement of employees into and out of an organization, over a given time period, usually a year; it is an indicator of how stable a business is. It is usually measured by the following formula:

$$\text{Labour turnover} = \frac{\text{Number of staff leaving over a year}}{\text{Average number of staff employed in a year}} \times 100$$

Although some labour turnover may be good for a business, a high labour turnover rate suggests that the business has labour problems, such as employees' dissatisfaction.

Methods of recruitment

Recruiting a new employee is a process composed of several steps:

1. **Preparation** of the job description and of the person specification

2. **Application** process, either through **internal recruitment** (when the organization recruits someone already working there; it can be a form of promotion and thus a reward) or **external recruitment** (recruiting new employees who are not already employed by the organization)

3. **Selection** of the candidates (which could be through interviews, tests etc)

>> **Revision tip**

For this sub-unit, you have to memorize some lists of abstract terms. You could create your own tricks (mnemonics) to do so, for example:

McClelland was an **A**mazing **A**merican **P**rofessor, his three motivation concepts start with AAP: **A**chievement, **A**ffiliation, **P**ower

or

In Deci and Ryan's theory, what are the main keywords? Take each other letter of their name: **D**e**C**i **R**y**A**n: **D**etermination (theory) and the three needs: **C**ompetence, **R**elatedness, **A**utonomy.

QUESTION PRACTICE

This question is about a hotel called Thorn Hills (*TH*) which is encountering problems of punctuality and absenteeism.

Using Herzberg's motivation theory, explain **one** reason for the recent issue at *TH* with punctuality and absenteeism. [2]

SAMPLE STUDENT ANSWER

Response 1

▲ The candidate shows their knowledge of Herzberg's hygiene factors and applies it well to the context of TH.

The employees of TH Function Room are on flexible contracts that do not cover what Herzberg calls "hygiene needs": no job security, no guaranteed hours of work, decreasing relationship with supervisors (as a consequence of the de-layering). They express their lack of motivation through their absenteeism and lack of punctuality.

This response could have achieved 2/2 marks.

QUESTION PRACTICE

This question is about an internet start-up business called Gen Y Limited, owned by Zack Johnson.

The employees are specialist programmers and coders who create innovative market research data reports.

Apply Deci and Ryan's self-determination motivation theory to the programmers at Gen Y. [6]

According to Deci and Ryan, employees have three motivational needs: autonomy, competence and relatedness.

Gen Y programmers have autonomy, especially to work on their own "dream projects" one day a week (so 20% of their time); this autonomy goes with the fact that they are empowered to make their own decisions, which is why Zack's "laissez-faire" leadership style is approproiate.

Gen Y programmers are all very competent – it is showed in their ability to be creative, which is essential in their industry. They know how to take risks in their work. They master their technical knowledge (programming) but other soft skills too – and they are clearly motivated by the job enlargement.

Gen Y programmers also have relatedness at work; they clearly enjoy working with their colleagues, which is also linked to "love and belonging" in Maslow's pyramid. Zack manages well to encourage this team spirit and collaboration through the team building games mentioned in the last paragraph.

▲ Each paragraph combines "theory" and "practice"; the candidate understands the three drivers (Autonomy, Mastery, Purpose) and applies them well to the case study with concise relevant examples.

This response could have achieved 6/6 marks.

QUESTION PRACTICE

This question is about a cleaning company called Green Clean (GC) whose cleaners are becoming demotivated, hence the question:

With reference to **two** motivation theories, examine the motivation of cleaners at GC. [10]

How should you select the two motivation theories for your answer?

1. Choose motivation theories that you know well: for example, if you do not remember by heart the names and order of the levels in Maslow's pyramid of needs, do not choose it.

2. All motivational theories may not be equally appropriate for the scenario given. The examiner will not penalize you for a poor choice, but it may make it harder for you to answer the question. In the case of GC cleaners, according to the stimulus material, the cleaners have always perceived their wages as fair. As a consequence, Adams' equity theory could be easily applied, especially if you consider the cleaners' feelings of unhappiness towards the newly appointed gardeners who have comparable skillsets but are paid much higher rates (hence a problem with the inputs/outputs equity).

If, in class, you have studied other motivation theories that are not in the IB syllabus (for example McGregor's Theory X and Theory Y, or Vroom's expectancy theory), you are allowed use them; you will not be penalized.

Content link
Link to other sub-units

- Sub-unit 2.3 about leadership and management is closely linked to this sub-unit about motivation, because leaders and managers must ensure that their employees remain well motivated in order to perform well.

- Sub-unit 3.3 about costs has close links to this sub-unit about motivation as all financial forms of motivation represent a cost for the organization (sometimes a fixed cost, in the case of a salary; sometimes a variable cost, in the case of a commission or profit-related pay).

Concept link

The concepts of **change** and **ethics** are linked to the topic of motivation:

- Employees' motivation may **change** over time; when it decreases (demotivation), managers may have recourse to different motivational techniques and rewards.

- Fairly rewarding employees is a matter of **ethics**, especially when comparing financial rewards in terms of parity. In many countries, women are still paid less than their male colleagues, even when they do the same job.

Content link
Link to your IA

Even if your IA is not specifically about human resources, you can apply the contents of this sub-unit to your chosen organization. What types of financial and non-financial rewards are used? Has it always been the case? Could there be sometimes problems of demotivation with some employees? What could cause this, and why? What could be done about it? Your IA gives you the chance to learn more about the contents of this sub-unit in context.

2.5 ORGANIZATIONAL (CORPORATE) CULTURE HL ONLY

This sub-unit focuses on the way organizations, like countries, have their own culture, with their own attitudes, beliefs and values.

You should be able to:

✔ define the term "organizational culture"

✔ explain the elements that make up the culture of an organization

✔ distinguish between types of organizational culture

✔ discuss the reasons for, and consequences of, cultural clashes within organizations, for example when they grow, merge, and when leadership styles change.

Test yourself

Describe the culture of three different organizations that you know.

HL Topic summary

The term **organizational culture** (sometimes called **corporate culture**) refers to the attitudes, experiences, beliefs and values of an organization – and the way all employees interact with one another, and with external stakeholders.

The culture of an organization is made up of many elements, such as its history and traditions, symbols and language used, norms and expectations. Many theorists have written about organizational culture, for example Handy's typology of "power culture", "role culture", "task culture" and "person culture". In his book *Gods of Management: The Changing Work of Organizations* (1995), Handy chose four Greek gods to symbolize those cultures: Zeus for "power culture", Apollo for "role culture", Athena for "task culture", and Dionysus for "person culture".

The culture of an organization could be described as conservative (traditional), international, entrepreneurial, innovative, etc. Organizational culture can change, rapidly or not; individuals (such as a new CEO) may influence the culture of the organization, just as the organizational culture influences all employees.

Culture clashes happen for many reasons, such as different degrees of formality, different practices, different senses of time – and can lead to many problems, such as higher labour turnover, conflict and decreased productivity.

Assessment tip

It is rare to have an exam question *solely* on the topic of organizational culture; however you may need to refer to it when you answer other questions. Even if the term "organizational culture" is not explicit in the question, always think about it.

 Content link

Link to other sub-units

Several sub-units are closely linked to this one:

- Sub-unit 1.5 about growth and evolution, as a merger will have an impact on the culture of the newly created organization (as the two companies merging may have different cultures, with the risk of culture clashes).

- Sub-unit 2.2 about organizational structure, as a change in the structure of the organization may have an impact on its culture, especially if the structure becomes taller or flatter.

- Sub-unit 2.3 about leadership and management, as for example the external appointment of a new CEO may have an impact on the culture of an organization.

Content link

Link to your IA

Even if your IA is not specifically about human resources, you can apply the contents of this sub-unit to your chosen organization. How would you describe the culture of the organization, and why? Your IA gives you the chance to learn more about the contents of this sub-unit in context.

Concept link

- The concept of **creativity** is relevant for this sub-unit, as some organizations have creativity as a core value, especially in the so-called creative industries (such as advertising, architecture, art, crafts, design, fashion, film, games, performing arts, publishing etc).

- How about the other three concepts (**change**, **ethics**, and **sustainability**); how can you link them to the topic of organizational culture?

2.6 COMMUNICATION

You should be able to:

✔ evaluate formal and informal methods of communication for an organization in a given situation

✔ explain barriers to communication.

This sub-unit introduces the topic of communication which is important in all departments of all organizations, in the private, public and voluntary sector.

Topic summary

- Communication within organizations and with all their stakeholders, internal and external, comes in several forms: verbal communication, visual communication and written communication.

- Formal communication refers to the official and formally recognized methods of communication, such as meetings, memos, emails etc.

- Informal communication refers to the ways in which information is casually and unofficially disseminated, including rumours and gossip.

- Many barriers to communication exist: communication styles (including personal preferences), linguistic and/or cultural barriers, lack of transparency, mistrust, psychological barriers, structural barriers etc. They can be very costly to businesses!

QUESTION PRACTICE

This question refers to a case study about a social enterprise called *Reach Out* whose mission is "to provide online support for families of children with autism and to offer them communication resources at a greatly reduced price".

Explain **two** barriers to communication at Reach Out.   [4]

SAMPLE STUDENT ANSWER

Response 1

▼ The first barrier is correct but not sufficiently applied to the case study.

> The first barrier to communication is the inability to listen to others: some people don't really listen to their colleagues or their customers. This happens in all organisations, including social enterprises like Reach Out.

▲ The second barrier is correct and sufficiently applied to the case study.

> The second problem is about language: some of the RO volunteers are from Eastern European countries (line 68), so maybe they don't speak English too well, or maybe they are fluent but they miss some of the subtleties when Neil Johnson talks to them. As a very educated businessman, he may not realise that the volunteers do not always understand him and his humour.

This response coud have achieved 3/4 marks.

 Content link

Link to your IA

Can you find out about the main methods of communication in your chosen organization? According to its size, they will be very different: a small organization may have more informal methods, whereas a very large one (such as an MNC) will have formal, bureaucratic channels of communication. You could also explore external visual communication: has the logo changed over the years? Do they use a website or social media networks to communicate to external stakeholders? All this is part of communication! Your IA gives you the chance to learn more about the contents of this sub-unit in context.

Content link

Link to other sub-units

This sub-unit is linked to many others, especially:

- Sub-unit 1.4, as communication is always about sharing information with stakeholders (internal or stakeholders);

- Sub-unit 2.7 (HL only), as some industrial conflicts are due to breakdown in communication at work;

- Sub-unit 4.6 (HL only), as international marketing requires slick communication across languages and cultures;

- Sub-unit 5.7 (HL only), as accurate, reliable and detailed communication facilitates the management of crises.

Concept link

This sub-unit is particularly linked to the concepts of **ethics** because communication must be truthful, which is essential in an era of fake news and misleading messages (including in promotional materials).

2.7 INDUSTRIAL/EMPLOYEE RELATIONS HL ONLY

You should be able to:

✔ explain common sources of conflict at work

✔ evaluate the main methods of industrial relations used by employers and by employees

✔ discuss the main approaches to conflict resolution at work.

This sub-unit focuses on the relations between employer and employee, especially regarding conflict and conflict resolution at work.

HL Topic summary

The relations between employers and employees (also called **industrial relations**) may sometimes be tense or difficult about the terms and conditions of employment, typically about pay, change taking place at work, different values and interests, insufficient resources and poor communication.

In larger organizations, employers and employees have **representatives** who are responsible for discussing and negotiating together in order to reach agreements and to avoid the creation and escalation of conflicts. These discussions are called **collective bargaining**. When collective bargaining is not successful:

- employees may go on strike, or may decide to "go slow", "work-to-rule" or refuse to work overtime

- employers may threaten employees with redundancy, with change of contract, or could close the workplace and lock the employees out.

Test yourself

Identify the advantages and disadvantages of the different types of action that may be taken by employees and by their employer, when collective bargaining fails and industrial dispute begins.

The main approaches to conflict resolution at work are:

- **conciliation and arbitration**, with the intervention of an independent third party

- **employee participation** and **industrial democracy**, involving employees more directly in decision-making, consultation or communication

- **no-strike agreement** by the trade union, so work will not completely stop

- **single-union agreement**, which means that the employer negotiates with only one trade union.

>> Assessment tip

Questions using the command term "define" are the only questions where you are *not* required to include examples or applications. They are always worth 2 marks, and you will score:

- 1 mark if you show *partial* knowledge and understanding of the term
- 2 marks if you show *good* knowledge and understanding of the term.

Example: Define the term "arbitration".

Response 1	Arbitration is a form of collective bargaining.	Incorrect answer: Arbitration is not a form of collective bargaining; it is an approach to conflict resolution. No mark can be awarded when the answer is not correct at all. **0 marks.**
Response 2	Arbitration is a method to resolve an industrial dispute when the employer and the workers cannot agree.	Partial answer: The candidate has some knowledge of what arbitration means, but an important idea is missing, about the intervention of the conciliator. **1 mark.**
Response 3	Arbitration is a method to resolve an industrial dispute when the employer and the employees cannot agree. It usually involves a neutral, independent third party who acts as conciliator and intermediary to help find a solution.	Full answer: The candidate's knowledge is good and correct. **2 marks.**

Although short answers may be comprehensive enough to be rewarded by 2 marks, it is always a good idea to develop your answer – and you have time to write more than one or two lines!

For your definitions, write a couple of sentences, or make two distinct points – that way, you show the examiner that your knowledge is sound and secure: if your answer is too short, you may give the impression that you do not know much (even if you do).

The examiner will reward your knowledge and understanding of the term, so do not worry if your definition feels a bit clumsy or not too elegantly formulated. Likewise, do not worry about spelling, grammar and punctuation; the examiner will not penalize you if you write "lockout" instead of "lock-out".

Content link
Link to other sub-units

- Sub-unit 2.3 about leadership and management is closely linked to this sub-unit because a manager's leadership style may be a source of conflict. For example, if an autocratic manager replaces one who had a more laissez-faire approach, the employees may be unhappy with the way they are now managed.

- Sub-unit 2.5 (HL only) about organizational culture is closely linked to this sub-unit because the culture of an organization influences industrial relations. Some companies may have a culture of recurrent dispute and conflicts between employer and employees, for example in the manufacturing and transportation sectors in some countries such as France.

- Sub-unit 5.7 (HL only) about crisis management is relevant as some cases of industrial conflict may require the organization to communicate to its stakeholders about what is happening.

Content link
Link to your IA

Even if your IA is not specifically about human resources, you can apply the contents of this sub-unit to your chosen organization. Have there been cases of tension or even open conflict at work, with industrial action? How are the relations between employer and employees usually handled? How is **change** managed in the organization? Your IA gives you the chance to learn more about the contents of this sub-unit in context.

Concept link

The concept of **change** is clearly linked to the topic of employer and employee relations, as relations between employer and employees keep changing over time, from periods of harmony to episodes of open conflict; the aim of collective bargaining is to anticipate and avoid these conflicts.

- How about **ethics**, **creativity** and **sustainability**? How can you link these three concepts to the topic of employer and employee relations?

3 FINANCE AND ACCOUNTS

You should know:

- ✔ Introduction to finance
- ✔ Sources of finance
- ✔ Costs and revenues
- ✔ Final accounts

- ✔ Profitability and liquidity ratio analysis
- ✔ Efficiency ratio analysis (HL only)
- ✔ Cash flow
- ✔ Investment appraisal
- ✔ Budgets (HL only)

3.1 INTRODUCTION TO FINANCE

This sub-unit introduces two key terms: capital expenditure and revenue expenditure.

You should be able to:

- ✔ explain the role of finance for businesses
- ✔ distinguish between **capital expenditure** and **revenue expenditure**.

Topic summary

All organizations need funding (finance): it could be to set up a business ("start-up costs"), to cover the day-to-day operations or for future growth and expansion.

- **Capital expenditure** is long-term investment: money spent to acquire **fixed assets** in a business, such as machinery, equipment, vehicles, buildings.

- **Revenue expenditure** is money used for the day-to-day operations of a business, for example purchasing raw materials, paying wages and energy bills.

 Assessment tip

The command term "distinguish" is defined as "Make clear the differences between two or more concepts or items" – so if an exam question asks you to "distinguish between capital expenditure and revenue expenditure", you must show that you understand the diffferences.

 Content link

Link to your IA

Once you have chosen your organization for your IA, you should ask yourself what "capital expenditure" and "revenue expenditure" mean for it: your IA gives you the chance to learn more about the contents of this sub-unit in context.

 Content link

Link to other sub-units

This sub-unit introduces Unit 3 in general, so it is relevant for all sub-units about Finance, especially sub-unit 3.2 about sources of finance.

3.2   SOURCES OF FINANCE

You should be able to:

✔ define short-term, medium-term and long-term finance

✔ distinguish between the three internal sources of finance: personal funds (for sole traders), retained profit, and sale of assets

✔ distinguish between the eight external sources of finance: share capital, loan capital, overdrafts, trade credit, crowdfunding, leasing, micro-finance provider, and business angels

✔ discuss the appropriateness, advantages and disadvantages of sources of finance for a given situation.

Topic summary

Sources of finance can be categorized as internal or external.

There are three **internal** sources of finance:

1. **Personal funds**: sole traders often use their own savings, sometimes with external sources of finance, for example to show a bank their personal commitment.

2. **Retained profit**: for an existing business (as opposed to a new start-up), this is what remains after payment of tax (to the government) and dividends (to the shareholders); it can be described as a form of reinvestment and is also called "ploughed-back profit".

3. **Sale of assets**: when the business sells unwanted or unused assets (for example obsolete machinery or vehicles) to raise funds.

There are eight **external** sources of finance:

1. **Share capital** (also known as "equity capital"): money raised from the sale of shares of a limited company; public limited companies sell their shares on the stock exchange.

2. **Loan capital** (also known as "debt capital"): money from a financial institution, such as a bank; it is repaid in instalments with interest (at a fixed rate or at a variable rate).

3. **Overdrafts**: when a lending institution (such as a bank) allows a business to spend or withdraw more money than it has on its account, for a short, temporary period of time.

4. **Trade credit**: an agreement between businesses that allows the buyer to pay the supplier a little later, such as one to three months.

5. **Crowdfunding:** funding by a large number of people, each contributing a small amount of money (also called crowd-sourcing).

6. **Leasing**: a source of finance that allows a firm to use an asset without purchasing it, but renting it, with periodic payment.

7. **Micro-finance providers**: institutions that provide banking services to low income or unemployed individuals or groups (who otherwise would not have access to financial services).

8. **Business angels**: rich individuals who invest in start-up enterprises in return for part-ownership and some control in their strategic development.

All sources of finance have advantages and disadvantages; each will be more or less appropriate for a given situation. When choosing a source of finance, several factors must be taken into consideration, especially:

- Duration: short term (repayment within 12 months); medium term (between 1 year and 5 years); long term (more than 5 years).
- Origin of funds (internal or external).
- Amount required.
- Level of flexibility.
- Purpose.

QUESTION PRACTICE

Utopia is a resort on the island of Ratu in the Pacific Ocean. Paul, the son of the owner, is considering developing the brand of *Utopia* by selling customized souvenirs produced by three-dimensional (3D) printers, which would cost $10 000.

With reference to *Utopia*, describe two suitable sources of finance for the 3D printers.   [4]

SAMPLE STUDENT ANSWER

Response 1

▲ This short introduction is useful; the candidate displays some promising knowledge of the subject (sources of finance) and names the two sources of finance that they will develop in their answer: retained profit and bank loan.

> Sources of finance are used to kickstart a business, and are separated into internal sources of finance and external sources of finance. The new 3D printer business could utilize retained profits and bank loans as suitable sources of finance.

▲ The first source of profit is briefly defined, then the candidate goes on to apply it to the case study ("Connecting it to *Utopia*…")

> First of all, retained profits are the money that the business earned from their previous year's operations.

▲ The candidate uses subject terminology (e.g. "capital expenditure") throughout their answer, always applying it to the situation.

> Connecting it to Utopia, as the 3D printing business is an extension for Utopia, John and Paul could utilize profits earned from Utopia before the natural disaster to cover all the costs for the 3D printing business. For example, they could use retained profits to pay for the $10 000 needed for capital expenditure and still possess enough cash for the daily running of the business.

▲ The next part starts with a new paragraph, which makes the answer easy to follow.

▲ The candidate shows that they understand that all sources of finance have advantages and disadvantages, but they justify their answer, with reference to the case study.

> Furthermore, the 3D printing business could ask for loans from banks that could be paid back after one year in the balance sheet. Loans from banks would ensure that the 3D printing possessed enough finance for the business to continue running for one more year. However, the Ariki family would need to take into account the interest rates charged by the banks as they would need to make sure that they have enough money to pay back the loan.

Note: The answer is very clear and contextualized: 2 marks for each suitable source of finance, well described with reference to *Utopia*, as required by the task.

This response could have achieved 4/4 marks.

>> **Assessment tip**

As in this answer, use business management terminology throughout. Here, the candidate used terms such as "capital expenditure", "balance sheet" and "interest rates". This is the vocabulary of our subject: show the examiner that you know these terms and that you can use them accurately; this will help you score higher marks. The Grade 7 descriptor includes the following feature: "a precise use of terminology which is specific to the subject".

SAMPLE STUDENT ANSWER

Response 2

One suitable source of finance for the 3D printers could be the external investors/stakeholders that wish to see the brand develop and to increase profit. Since they function with Utopia's best interest in mind, out of the many external finance sources, costs could be covered quickly. Another suitable source of finance would be internal finances, since John refuses to grow any business through external finance, he can finance for 3D printers through retained profit, out of his own personal funds, loans and so on. Both of these finance sources would be a suitable option to fund the 3D printers.

▼ The first part of the answer is vague ("external investors/stakeholders") and confusing: "stakeholders" are not a source of finance; maybe the candidate meant "shareholders" – but then they are not external.

▲ The second part of the answer includes the terms "retained profit" and "loans" which are two acceptable sources – even if the answer is a little confusing, as the candidate seems to consider them together, as one single source, but the examiner is giving the candidate the benefit of the doubt.

Note: Two suitable sources are identified overall (retained profit and loans), but not developed.

This response could have achieved 2/4 marks.

 Content link
Link to your IA

Even if your IA is not specifically about finance and accounts, you can apply the contents of this unit to your chosen organization. What sources of finance do they normally use? Why? Has it always been the case? Your IA gives you the chance to learn more about the contents of this unit in context.

 Content link
Link to other sub-units

*   This sub-unit introduces unit 3 in general, so all other sub-units 3.3 to 3.9 are linked to it.

>> **Assessment tip**

You may be asked about the suitability of a particular source of finance; use your critical thinking skills. For example, overdrafts would not be suitable to purchase a vehicle, but leasing would be.

Concept link

The concept of **change** is linked to the topic of sources of finance because a business will have access to different sources of finance over time. When they set up their business, many entrepreneurs use their personal funds; retained profit and sales of assets are not available at this point. Established organizations, on the other hand, have access to different sources of finance, such as retained profit (reinvestment) and equity capital.

3.3   COSTS AND REVENUES

This sub-unit examines the different types of costs paid by all organizations, and the revenue streams that help them determine their profit.

You should be able to:

✔ distinguish between the different types of costs

✔ explain how various revenue streams contribute to the total revenue of a business and therefore to its profit.

Topic summary

Costs can be:

- direct or indirect
- fixed or variable.

▼ Table 3.3.1 Costs overview

Direct costs	Costs linked to the production of specific goods and services (and thus to a specific "**cost centre**").	Examples: raw materials, direct labour, packaging costs.
Indirect costs	Costs that cannot be linked to the production of specific goods and services – also called "**overheads**".	Examples: rent, general administrative expenses, insurance, maintenance, cleaning and security.
Fixed costs	Do not change with the amount of goods or services produced.	Examples: rent/mortgage, insurance, salaries, interest payments.
Variable costs	Change with the amount of goods or services produced.	Examples: raw material costs, sales commission, packaging, energy usage costs.

Some costs are composed of both fixed and variable elements; they are called "**semi-variable costs**" (or "semi-fixed costs" or "mixed costs") – for example in the case of a reward package composed of "fixed salary + overtime" or "fixed salary + commission".

Total costs (TC) = total of fixed costs (TFC) + total of variable costs (TVC)

The main **revenue** of a business is usually the income from its trading activities, i.e. the income gained from the sale of goods and services, also called "sales revenue", "sales turnover", "turnover". It is calculated by multiplying the price per unit by the quantity of goods sold.

The **total revenue** of a business could have other streams (components):

- Rental income (the income from renting its properties, maybe seasonally).
- Sale of fixed assets (especially if they are unused or underused).
- Dividends (if it owns shares in another business).
- Donations, grants, subsidies.

>> **Assessment tip**

In daily language, many people talk about **revenue** and **profit** as being the same – but they are not:

- Revenue is the money generated by the sale of goods and services.
- Profit is calculated by total revenue minus total costs (TC).

The revenue of a business might be very high, but if the costs are very high too, the business might not be profitable!

Another common mistake is to mix the terms **cost** and **price**:

- Cost is the expense incurred for a product sold by a company (it includes direct and indirect costs, from the purchase of raw materials and direct labour, to contribution to overheads such as insurance, cleaning and security).
- Price is the amount charged to the customer (it may be calculated from the cost itself, for example with a mark-up, or using a different pricing strategy, for example based on competitors' prices).

When you use these words in your answers to business management exam questions, be careful.

Test yourself

Can you state examples of costs that are:

- direct and variable
- direct and fixed
- indirect and variable
- indirect and fixed.

>> **Assessment tip**

Common questions about this topic tend to use the command term "define", such as:

Define the term *variable* costs. [2]

Someone who has never studied business management might simply say "costs that vary" – but in a business management exam, this is not enough. In your answer, you must be more technical, stating that the variation depends on the level of output.

🔗 **Content link**

Link to your IA

Even if your IA is not specifically about finance and accounts, you can apply the contents of this unit to your chosen organization:

- What are its main streams of revenue? Have they changed over time? Could you suggest one more possible stream of revenue for the organization?
- What are its main cost centres?

Your IA gives you the chance to learn more about the contents of this sub-unit in context.

Content link

Link to other sub-units

- Sub-units 3.3 and 3.7 are closely linked because costs and revenue are key elements in a cash flow.

- Sub-units 3.3 and 4.5 are closely linked, because costs and prices are often wrongly taken as synonymous; the calculation of costs is explained in 3.3, whereas the setting of prices is explained in 4.5.

- Sub-units 3.3 and 5.5 are closely linked because fixed costs and variable costs play a key role in the calculation of break-even.

Concept link

The concept of **change** is linked to the topic of costs and revenues because costs and revenue streams are all subject to change. By nature, variable costs change according to the level of output, whereas fixed costs do not. Revenue also changes, according to the volume of sales and other factors (e.g. discounts) which means that profit always fluctuates too.

3.4   FINAL ACCOUNTS SOME HL ONLY

This sub-unit focuses on two types of financial statements used by businesses: profit and loss accounts (P&L) and balance sheets.

You should be able to:

✔ explain the purpose of accounts to different stakeholders

✔ prepare and interpret:

  ✔ the profit and loss account (P&L account) of a business

  ✔ the balance sheet of a business

✔ distinguish between types of intangible assets

✔ calculate depreciation using two methods (straight line and units of production) (HL only)

✔ evaluate the appropriateness of each method (HL only).

Topic summary

Numerous stakeholders need to know the financial statements of a business:

- Shareholders, because the dividends they receive is calculated from the profit and loss account.

- The government, because the profit and loss account helps to calculate the taxes that the business will have to pay.

- Potential investors and financiers, because they will want to know about the creditworthiness and financial health of the business to decide whether to invest in it... or not!

- Managers, because final accounts help them monitor performance, comparing the results to previous years, and set budgets and strategies.

- Employees, because a profitable business means that their job is secure, or that they could get a pay rise.

The **profit and loss account** (also called **income statement**) shows the records of income and expenditure over a period, typically a year. It includes data (such as **gross profit** and **net profit**) and eventually indicates if the business has made a **profit** or a **loss**. In the case of a profit, it shows how this profit is distributed (e.g. payment of **dividends** to shareholders, or **retained profit**). For non-profit making organizations, the "profit" is called "**surplus**".

The **balance sheet** (also called **statement of financial position**) indicates the assets, liabilities and equity of a firm at a specific date (this is the same for profit-making and non-profit-making organizations).

- The **assets** are what the company owns: **fixed assets** (long-term, such as buildings or vehicles) and **current assets** (lasting less than a year: stock/inventory, current cash, and money owed by debtors).

- The **liabilities** are what the company owes: **long-term liabilities** (such as a bank loan) and **current liabilities** (short-term debts to be paid within a year, money owed to creditors, tax payable to the government).

In the context of a balance sheet, the term **equity** refers to the amount of money that would be returned to a business if all of the assets were liquidated.

Liquidation is a situation where all the assets are sold off in order to pay off the debts of an organization.

The balance sheet makes it possible to calculate the **working capital** ("net current assets"):

Working capital = total current assets – total current liabilities

Another important calculation is the net assets of a business:

Net assets = total assets – current liabilities – long-term liabilities

The net assets correspond to the **equity** of a business, indicating how the assets were financed (**share capital** from shareholders and **retained profit**).

Besides the "fixed assets" and "current assets" of a business, there is a third type of "assets": **intangible assets**. These are not physical, cannot easily be quantified and showed on a balance sheet, even though they add value to a business. The four main **intangible assets** are trademarks, patents, goodwill and copyright.

HL **Depreciation** is the decrease in the value of a fixed asset over time.

The two main causes of depreciation are:

- Wear and tear (for example for vehicles or machinery, as their repeated use means that their value decreases over time).

- Obsolescence (for example computer hardware and software that fall in value as new or improved products are commercialized).

This is recorded in the profit and loss account as an expense. It can be calculated in two ways:

(1) Using the **straight line method**. This method is commonly used as it is simple to calculate. The cost is equally spread over the lifetime of the asset, using the following formula:

$$\text{Annual depreciation} = \frac{\text{original cost} - \text{residual value}}{\text{expected life of asset}}$$

Every year, it is the same amount which is counted as annual depreciation expense.

(2) Using the **units of production method** (also called units of activity method), basing depreciation not on time (number of years) but on usage (so an asset which is used a lot will depreciate faster than an asset used less often).

Example of a 3D printer with an original cost of $30 000 and a salvage (final) value of $6000:

(1) To use the **straight line method**, we need to know the duration of the asset, for example 4 years: its annual depreciation is then $6000 per year: $\frac{(30\,000 - 6000)}{4}$. This can be shown in the following table, with the same depreciation expense every year; there is however no information about how intensively the 3D printer is used and how many units are produced.

▼ **Table 3.4.1** Calculating depreciation using the straight line method

Year	Straight line depreciation	
	Annual depreciation expense	Net book value
0	0	$30 000
1	$6000	$24 000
2	$6000	$18 000
3	$6000	$12 000
4	$6000	$6000

(2) To use the **units of production methods**, we need to know how many units are produced, for example 10 000 units; the depreciation expense can then be calculated as follows:

$$\text{Units of production rate} = \frac{(\text{original cost} - \text{salvage value})}{\text{units of production}}$$

$$\text{Units of production rate} = \frac{(30\,000 - 6000)}{10\,000} = 2.4$$

Depreciation expense = units of production rate × units produced

Depreciation expense = 2.4 × 10 000 = 24 000

In this case, we know the amount of the depreciation expense ($24 000), once the 3D printer has produced 10 000 units, but we do not know how long this may take. If the 3D printer is used very intensively, it may reach 10 000 units at the end of two years; in this case, it will be depreciated by $24 000 at the end of two years, so $12 000 a year. If the 3D printer is hardly ever used, it could take

10 years and the yearly amount of depreciation would then be much lower. In fact, the 3D printer may be used differently each year, even each month and each day!

The second method (calculating depreciation based on units of production) writes down an asset based on its usage as opposed to time. It is more accurate, as it reflects the declining physical value of an asset over time (wear and tear); however, it is more difficult to calculate: it requires some data that may not easily be calculated in advance.

>> **Revision tip**

Questions about final accounts are usually asked in every Paper 2 exam, so make sure you know how to approach these questions. It is essential that you know the exact order of the elements in the two final accounts (profit and loss; balance sheet). The IB has specific presentation requirements for these accounts; you must learn them and follow them. There are other presentation methods in some books, and some national systems are slightly different too.

>> **Assessment tip**

Questions about final accounts usually only require you to provide numbers and tables, unless you are also asked to interpret the data, i.e. to write some text to explain what they mean.

QUESTION PRACTICE

Sotatsu Electronics (SE)

Sotatsu Electronics (*SE*) manufactures electronic products and is famous for its innovative televisions. In late 2025, *SE* introduced a new high-definition television with twice the quality of the best-selling television of its chief competitor. Determining that it would be two years before its competitors could have a similar product, *SE* adopted a price skimming strategy.

Table 1: Select financial information for *SE* for 2025 and 2026. Figures in $000 000.

	2025	2026
Cash	300	250
Cost of goods sold	2100	2300
Creditors	180	230
Expenses	1200	1300
Fixed assets	1075	1275
Gross profit	X	2800
Net profit before interest and tax	1000	Y
Sales revenue	4300	5100
Total current assets	650	700
Total current liabilities	275	300

(...)

a) i) Calculate the values of **X** and **Y** in Table 1 (*no working required*). [2]

ii) Construct a profit and loss account for *SE* for 2025 **and** 2026. [4]

b) Calculate net current assets (working capital) for 2026 (*show all your working*). [2]

a i)

X = Gross profit in 2025

Gross profit = sales revenue – costs of goods sold = 4300 – 2100

= 2200

X = $2 200 000 000

Y = Net profit before interest and tax in 2026

Net profit before interest and tax = gross profit – expenses

Net profit before interest and tax = 2800 – 1300 = 1500

Y = $1 500 000 000

▲ The results are correct. The candidate included the workings (i.e. the details of how they did their calculations). This was not necessary, it would have been enough to write the values of **X** and **Y**.

This response could have achieved 2/2 marks.

>> **Assessment tip**

Remember to add the unit at the end. This is very important for all your calculation results: $2200 is not the same as 2200 or 2200%.

a ii)

	2025	2026
Sales revenue	4300	5100
Costs of goods sold	2100	2300
Gross profit	2200	2800
Expenses	1200	1300
Net profit before interest and tax	1000	1500

(All figures in $000 000)

The profit and loss accounts are correct.

This response could have achieved 4/4 marks.

b)

Working capital = total current assets – total current liabilities

700 – 300 = 400

Net current assets (working capital) in 2016 = $400 000 000

▲ The result is correct – and this time, the workings *were* required.

This response could have achieved 2/2 marks.

Geo Dynamics (GD)

Geo Dynamics (GD) is an engineering company. On 1 January 2023, *GD* purchased new machinery at a cost of $50 000 rather than leasing it. *GD*'s financial manager researched further information:

- The machinery has a useful life of four years.

- Its residual or scrap value will be $8000.

- The engineering industry uses a 40% depreciation rate per annum.

- Technology in this industry is changing rapidly.

GD's financial manager has not yet decided on which depreciation method (such as straight line or reducing/declining balance) to use for the new machinery.

a) Calculate the value (also known as net book value) of new machinery at 31 December 2024 using the straight line depreciation method (*show all your working*). [2]

b) Explain **one** advantage for *GD* of using the straight line balance depreciation method. [2]

SAMPLE STUDENT ANSWER

a)

$$\text{Annual depreciation} = \frac{\text{purchase cost} - \text{residual value}}{\text{life span}}$$

$$\frac{50000 - 8000}{4} = 10500 \text{ per year}$$

$$10500 \times 2 = 21000$$

$$50000 - 21000 = 29000$$

By the end of 2024, it will have a book value of $29000

> This answer is correct.

This response could have achieved 2/2 marks.

b) An advantage is the fact that the higher amount of depreciation in the first year is more realistic, as machinery and vehicles usually lose more value in the early years than later on.

> ▼ The candidate did not precisely answer the question. What they write is correct but it is not clearly explained as an advantage of using the straight line balance depreciation method. Although the answer shows knowledge and understanding, well applied here, they cannot score any marks, as they did not answer the question asked, but another one.

This response could have achieved 0/2 marks.

Content link
Link to your IA

Even if your IA is not specifically about finance and accounts, you can apply the contents of this sub-unit to your chosen organization. Can you get hold of their P&L accounts and their balance sheets? Their financial statements may be more complicated than the models used here, and the terminology may be slightly different, but the principles are the same. Your IA gives you the chance to learn more about the contents of this sub-unit in context.

Content link
Link to other sub-units

- Sub-units 3.4 and 3.5 are closely linked because some of the data in the final accounts make it possible to calculate profitability and liquidity ratios.

- Sub-units 3.4 and 3.6 (HL only) are closely linked because some of the data in the final accounts make it possible to calculate efficiency ratios.

Concept link

The concept of **ethics** is linked to the topic of final accounts because accountants should have a high standard of ethics. The ACCA (Association of Chartered Certified Accountants), the international body for professional accountants, has a "Code of Ethics and Conduct" which is binding for all its members who must commit themselves to follow the five principles of integrity (honesty), objectivity, professional competence, confidentiality and professional behaviour.

3.5 PROFITABILITY AND LIQUIDITY RATIO ANALYSIS

This sub-unit focuses on five financial ratios calculated from financial statements.

You should be able to:

✔ calculate and interpret three profitability ratios: the gross profit margin; the profit margin; and the return on capital employed: ROCE

✔ discuss possible strategies to improve these ratios

✔ calculate and interpret two liquidity ratios: current ratio and acid-test (quick) ratio

✔ discuss possible strategies to improve these ratios.

Topic summary

The first two **profitability ratios** help assess the performance of a business based on its ability to generate profit. They use data from the profit and loss account.

Gross profit margin (GPM)

$$\text{Gross profit margin} = \frac{\text{gross profit}}{\text{sales revenue}} \times 100$$

Profit margin (PM) sometimes called Net profit margin (NPM)

$$\text{Profit margin} = \frac{\text{net profit before interest and tax}}{\text{sales revenue}} \times 100$$

Several strategies may help improve GPM, for example increasing prices (to increase sales revenue) or trying to find cheaper suppliers (to decrease the cost of goods sold). To improve PM, the business could also try to reduce expenses (for example overheads).

The **ratio ROCE** helps measure how well a business utilizes its assets and liabilities. It uses data from the balance sheet to assess the returns a business is making from its capital employed.

$$\text{Return on capital employed (ROCE)} = \frac{\text{profit before interest and tax}}{\text{capital employed}} \times 100$$

Capital employed = long-term liabilities + share capital + retained profit

Several strategies may help improve ROCE, for example the business could pay more dividends to shareholders, reducing the retained profit and thus increasing ROCE.

The **liquidity ratios** measure the ability of a business to pay off its short-term debts, i.e. how quickly current assets could be converted into "liquid" cash. They use data from the balance sheet.

Current ratio

$$\text{Current ratio} = \frac{\text{current assets}}{\text{current liabilities}}$$

Acid test (quick) ratio

$$\text{Acid test (quick) ratio} = \frac{\text{current assets} - \text{stock}}{\text{current liabilities}}$$

As a rule of thumb, these ratios should be around 1.5. Low ratios (under 1) mean that the business could struggle to pay off its debts. High ratios (above 2) should be avoided too, as they could mean that there is too much cash being held unnecessarily and not invested, or that there are too many debtors. These numbers, however, vary across industries and are also linked to speed of stock turnover: retail, for example, may not need as high a current ratio or acid test ratio.

Several strategies may help improve the liquidity ratios. The business could try to increase current assets and/or decrease current liabilities, or both. Selling off the stock at a discount is another possibility.

QUESTION PRACTICE

AFA was at a critical point. Sam and Finn had not fully resolved their disagreements. They seemed to be constantly arguing but Sam could also see that new issues were emerging. At their most recent meeting in early 2023, Finn provided the following financial information to illustrate the declining trend in gross profit margin.

Table 1: Selected financial information for *AFA*

Year	Gross profit	Sales revenue
2021	142 888	2 164 486
2022	124 211	2 400 625

(...)

a) i) Calculate the gross profit margin of *AFA* for 2021 **and** 2022.   [2]

    ii) Explain one possible reason for the trend in gross profit margin for *AFA* between 2021 and 2022.   [2]

» Assessment tip

Questions about ratios are asked often in paper 2 exams; there is usually *at least one* in each exam session, so make sure you know how to approach these questions. They usually have two parts:

- Firstly, you are asked to calculate some ratios, applying the formulae (which are provided on a formulae sheet).

- Secondly, you are asked to interpret your findings, i.e. to write some text to explain what the ratios mean for the business, hence the word "ratio analysis".

The two results are correct.

▼ The candidate does not answer the question about a possible reason. They repeat the numbers that they have just calculated and comment on the fact that it is a negative indicator, but this is not the question asked. The candidate should have commented on a likely cause: the fact that direct costs have risen faster than sales revenues (that have increased).

SAMPLE STUDENT ANSWER

a) i)

$$GPM\ 2021 = \frac{142\,888}{2\,164\,486} \times \frac{100}{1} = 6.6\%$$

$$GPM\ 2022 = \frac{124\,211}{2\,400\,625} \times \frac{100}{1} = 5.17\%$$

This response could have achieved 2/2 marks.

ii) Gross profit margin went down between 2021 and 2022, from 6.6% down to 5.12%, which is not a good sign, especially as the text states that it is a trend.

This response could have achieved 0/2 marks.

Content link
Link to other sub-units

Sub-units 3.5 and 3.4 are closely linked because the profitability and liquidity ratios are calculated from data found in the final accounts.

Content link
Link to your IA

Even if your IA is not specifically about finance and accounts, you can apply the contents of this sub-unit to your chosen organization. If you can have access to their profit and loss account and their balance sheet, do some calculations to practise your ratio calculation skills. Try to interpret your results, bearing in mind that all ratios must be interpreted in context.

Concept link

The concept of **change** is linked to the topic of profitability and liquidity ratios because ratio analysis only becomes meaningful when you compare changes and trends over several years, and across companies in the same sector. A ratio on its own does not mean much; for example, it is not possible to say if a gross profit margin of 10% is good or bad. This number must be compared to the gross profit margin of the previous years and to the gross profit margin of other businesses in the same sector in order to interpret it.

3.6 EFFICIENCY RATIO ANALYSIS HL ONLY

You should be able to:

✔ calculate and interpret four other efficiency ratios:

1) the stock (inventory) turnover ratio

2) the debtor (trade receivable) days ratio

3) the creditor days ratio

4) the gearing ratio

✔ discuss possible strategies to improve these ratios

✔ distinguish between insolvency and bankruptcy.

This sub-unit focuses on four efficiency ratios calculated from the balance sheet.

Topic summary

There are four other efficiency ratios that help assess how well a business uses its resources, assets and liabilities:

1. The **stock (inventory) turnover ratio** that measures how quickly the stock is sold and replaced. It may be calculated in two ways: how many times a year, or how many days it takes to replenish the stock:

$$\text{Stock turnover (number of times)} = \frac{\text{cost of goods sold}}{\text{average stock}}$$

or

$$\text{Stock turnover (number of days)} = \frac{\text{average stock}}{\text{cost of goods sold}} \times 365$$

There are several strategies to improve stock turnover ratio, such as adopting a "JIT" (Just in Time) production method.

2. The **debtor ("trade receivable", "debt collection") days ratio** about the number of days it takes a business to collect its debts from the customers who have paid on credit, and thus owe money to the business.

$$\text{Debtor days ratio (number of days)} = \frac{\text{debtors}}{\text{total sales revenue}} \times 365$$

There are several strategies to lower debtor days ratio, such as giving incentives to debtors to pay their debts early, or fining late payers.

3. The **creditor days ratio** about the number of days it takes a business to pay its own debts to its creditors (e.g. to its suppliers).

$$\text{Creditor days ratio (number of days)} = \frac{\text{creditors}}{\text{cost of goods sold}} \times 365$$

Possible strategies to increase creditor days ratio include negotiating extra time with suppliers ("trade credit").

4. The **gearing ratio** measures the extent to which the capital employed by a business is financed from loan capital. Put another way, this is the level of debt of a business. A "highly geared" business (with a ratio of 50% or above) is seen as risky by current shareholders and potential investors.

$$\text{Gearing ratio} = \frac{\text{loan capital}}{\text{capital employed}} \times 100$$

capital employed = loan capital (or long-term liabilities) + share capital + retained profit

Possible strategies to reduce gearing ratio include seeking sources of finance other than a loan, for example issuing more shares.

The terms "insolvency" and "bankruptcy" are closely linked; however, there is a difference. **Insolvency** refers to the **financial** state of a person or a firm that cannot pay its debts on time: they are not "solvent". In many cases, formally declaring **bankruptcy** is the next stage: it is the start of a **legal** process which usually involves the sale of all the assets in order to pay off the debts. The aim is to "liquidate" the assets i.e. to convert them into cash as soon as possible.

QUESTION PRACTICE

Bart Furniture (BF)

Bart Furniture (BF) is a wholesaler that stocks furniture. In 2021, *BF* purchased more stock than usual in order to take advantage of discounts that several furniture manufacturers were offering. However, much of this new stock did not sell.

Table 1: Financial information, for *BF*, for 2020 and 2021

	2020	2021
Acid-test/quick ratio	2.21	2.84
Cash	$2000	$500
Cost of goods sold	$12 166	$12 500
Creditors	$1000	$1438
Current ratio	**A**	5.47
Debtor days	30 days	**Y**
Debtors	$1973	$6134
Long-term debt	$14 000	$13 700
Sales revenue	$24 000	$26 000
Short-term debt	$800	$900
Stock	$4000	$6164
Stock turnover in days	**X**	180

(…)

a) Using information in **Table 1**, calculate for *BF*:

    i) stock turnover in days for 2020 (**X**) (*show all your working*);   [2]

    ii) debtor days for 2021 (**Y**) (*show all your working*).   [2]

SAMPLE STUDENT ANSWER

▼ The answer 120 is numerically correct but the candidate did not include the unit "days".

a) i)

$$\text{Stock turnover} = \frac{\text{average stock}}{\text{costs of goods sold}} \times 365$$

$$\frac{4000}{12166} \times 365 = 120$$

This response could have achieved 1/2 marks.

ii)

86 days

▼ The answer is numerically correct, but the candidate did not show their working, although this was required.

This response could have achieved 1/2 marks.

Revision tip

For questions about efficiency ratios, you need to use data from the balance sheet, so make sure you understand the elements of a balance sheet well, including their exact order. The IB has specific presentation requirements for the balance sheet, which may be slightly different from the balance sheet in your country and in some of your books. You must learn and follow the IB presentation of the balance sheet.

Content link
Link to your IA

Even if your IA is not specifically about finance and accounts, you can apply the contents of this unit to your chosen organization. If you can have access to their balance sheet, do some calculations about their efficiency ratios and try to interpret your findings, bearing in mind that all ratios must be interpreted in context.

Content link
Link to other sub-units

- Sub-units 3.6 and 3.4 are closely linked because the efficiency ratios are calculated from data found in the balance sheet.

- Sub-units 3.6 and 5.6 (HL only) are linked because one of the strategies to improve stock turnover ratio is the product method JIT (just-in-time) explained in 5.6.

- Sub-units 3.6 and 3.2 are linked because one of the strategies to increase creditor days ratio is trade credit, i.e. an agreement with suppliers to pay them later, as defined in 3.2, and strategies to reduce gearing ratio include seeking sources of finance other than a loan, for example issuing more shares, also defined in 3.2.

Concept link

The concept of **change** is linked to the topic of efficiency ratios because these ratios, like the other financial ratios, are only meaningful when you take the context into account, the norms in the sector and the evolution of the ratios over a period of time: ratio analysis is all about observing how ratios change, interpreting these changes, drawing conclusions and formulating recommendations for the business.

3.7   CASH FLOW

This sub-unit focuses on an important financial planning tool: cash flow forecast.

You should be able to:

✔ distinguish between profit and cash flow

✔ explain working capital and liquidity position

✔ construct and interpret cash flow forecasts

✔ analyse the relationship between investment, profit and cash flow

✔ discuss strategies to deal with cash flow problems.

Topic summary

Profit is the positive difference between sales revenue and total costs; it includes *both* cash transactions *and* credit transactions.

Cash flow is money that flows in and out of a business over a given period of time; it *only* includes cash transactions, not credit transactions. As defined in sub-unit 3.6, insolvency is when a business runs out of cash, even though it may still be profitable: it is a liquidity position without enough cash to run the day-to-day operations (i.e. to cover the revenue expenditure, as defined in sub-unit 3.1).

The **working capital** is calculated using data from the balance sheet: current assets minus current liabilities. It refers to money available straightaway to pay for revenue expenditure.

A **cash flow forecast** is a financial document in the form of a table that shows the predicted cash inflows and cash outflows, usually month by month:

▼ Table 3.7.1 Cash flow forecast with typical items of cash inflows and cash outflows

	Month 1	Month 2	Month 3
Opening balance	X	Y	Z
Cash inflows			
– Cash sales revenue			
– Tax refunds			
Total cash inflows	A		
Cash outflows			
Rent			
Packaging			
Salaries and wages			
Cost of sales			
Heating and lighting			
Delivery			
Total cash outflows	B		
Net cash flow	A – B		
Closing balance	Y = X + (A – B)	Z	

Note: This example is a monthly cash flow; however each period could be shorter or longer, for example days or quarters.

The relationship between investment, profit and cash flow varies at different stages of a business. A new business usually requires a lot of investment (to purchase the first fixed assets) but there is no profit yet, and cash flow is negative. An established business, on the other hand, requires less investment, but achieves more profit, with a positive cash flow.

There are three main strategies to deal with cash flow problems:

- **Reducing cash outflows** (for example delaying the purchase of some fixed assets, delaying payment of suppliers or sourcing cheaper suppliers).

- **Improving cash inflows** (for example limiting delayed payment on credit).

- **Looking for additional finance** (for example arranging a bank overdraft or selling some assets and leasing them back) as outlined in sub-unit 3.2.

Cash flow forecasts have several advantages. Like budgets, they are useful planning tools, providing estimated projections. They cannot however take into account unexpected changes in the economy, in competitors' strategies, or in other external factors.

QUESTION PRACTICE

Anubis

Tom operates *Anubis* as a sole trader, selling cell/mobile phone cases on the internet. The market is very competitive. The retail price of phone cases is predicted to fall in the second quarter of 2022. Employees at *Anubis* will receive a 3% rise in wages starting from 1 April 2022.

Tom has forecasted the following monthly cash outflows for January through March 2022:

- Heating and lighting: $4000.
- Wages: $50 000.
- Packaging: $15 000.
- Delivery charges: 5% of sales revenue.
- Cost of goods sold: $220 000.

Additional information:

- Opening balance on 1 January 2022: $8000.
- Sales revenue: $300 000 each month.
- Rent of $2000 paid quarterly: first payment in January 2022.
- Receipt of a tax refund in February 2022: $3000.

(...)

a) Using the information above, prepare a fully labelled cash flow forecast for *Anubis* from January to March 2022. [5]

b) Comment on the predicted cash flow for *Anubis* for 2022. [3]

a)

	January	February	March
Opening balance	8000	2000	1000
Inflows:			
Sales revenue	300000	300000	300000
Tax refund		3000	
TOTAL INFLOWS	300000	303000	300000
Outflows:			
Electricity	4000	4000	4000
Wages	50000	50000	50000
Packages	15000	15000	15000
Costs of goods sold	220000	220000	220000
Delivery charges	15000	15000	15000
5% of sales revenue			
Rent	2000		
TOTAL OUTFLOWS	306000	304000	304000
NET CASH FLOW	−6000	−1000	−4000
Closing balance	2000	1000	3000

▼ There is one error at the end, when the candidate calculated the closing balance for March: it is a negative closing balance of −3000 (minus 3000). The omission of the minus sign is very important in cash flow forecasts! It looks like the candidate calculated 4000 − 1000 = 3000 instead of 1000 − 4000 = −3000

Note: The table is good overall, the candidate clearly understands key principles of a cash flow forecast.

This response could have achieved 4/5 marks.

▲ The candidate rightfully interprets that, overall, the cash flow forecast is a cause for concern, and makes valid points about the ongoing trend and what may happen in April.

▲ For an even higher mark, the answer should be even more developed, for example noting that the business faces a lower gross profit margin, and that action is necessary to deal with the impending cash flow problems, for example reducing cash outflows, maybe on packages by finding cheaper suppliers (the packages represent 5% of sales revenue, which is a lot).

b) The cash flow forecast is worrying because the opening balance keeps decreasing, which is not a good indicator. Based on the trend of January, February and March, the following months will probably be worse. Wages in April will be higher (+3%) and there will also be rent to pay again, so with more cash outflows, April will be a difficult month for Anubis.

This response could have achieved 2/3 marks.

>> Assessment tip

Questions about cash flows are asked often in paper 2, so make sure you know how to approach them. In most cases, you will be given a list of facts and data and asked to construct a table. You could also be given a cash flow forecast for a given period, for example three months, and asked to prepare the cash flow forecast for the following two months. You must remain vigilant as the transactions are not always the same every month; for example some expenses may take place quarterly (every three months); or there might be a delay in cash flows in or out, for example if some of the customers do not pay at once, but next month. Go through all the information very slowly, when you construct your cash flow forecast.

>> **Assessment tip**

Cash flow and profit are different financial parameters that some candidates (and some business owners!) mix up. Make sure that you understand the difference and that you use the terms correctly. Positive cash flows are not profit. Profit is the difference between sales revenue and all costs (i.e. all expenses), whereas a positive cash flow simply means that more cash went in than out. A business can have a positive cash flow and yet *no profit* if the cash comes from sources other than income, for example if the owner puts some of their own money into the business. These transactions will be inflows in a cash flow table; however they are not income from sales revenue.

Content link

Link to your IA

Even if your IA is not specifically about finance and accounts, you can apply the contents of this unit to your chosen organization. What type of cash flow forecast do they use? It may be more elaborate than the simple model used here, but the principles are the same.

Content link

Link to other sub-units

- Sub-units 3.7 and 3.3 are linked as cash flow forecasts are based on costs and revenue streams.

- Sub-units 3.7 and 3.4 are linked as final accounts and cash flow forecasts should be read and interpreted together: they offer complementary information about financial aspects of the business.

Concept link

Like all topics of finance, cash flow forecasts are well analysed through the conceptual lens of **change**, especially as cash inflows and outflows keep changing.

3.8 INVESTMENT APPRAISAL SOME HL ONLY

You should be able to:

✔ calculate and evaluate investment opportunities using payback period and average rate of return (ARR)

✔ calculate and evaluate investment opportunities using net present value (NPV) (HL only).

This sub-unit focuses on quantitative techniques used to evaluate the viability and attractiveness of an investment proposal.

Topic summary

Investment is the act of spending money to purchase a **fixed asset** with the expectation of future earnings. Investment appraisals are techniques that can help with deciding the suitability of an investment opportunity: financially, can the expenditure be justified? These techniques are also useful to compare competing investment opportunities. They can be combined to help decision-making.

The **payback period** refers to the length of time required for an investment project to pay back its initial cost outlay. It is expressed in years and months.

$$\text{Payback period} = \frac{\text{Initial investment}}{\text{Annual cash flow from investment}}$$

The payback period method has several advantages, especially the fact that it is simple and fast to calculate. It also has disadvantages, especially the fact that it ignores the overall profitability of an investment beyond its payback.

The **average rate of return (ARR)**, also called "accounting rate of return", measures the annual net return of an investment, as a percentage of its capital cost.

$$\text{Average rate of return (ARR)} = \frac{(\text{total returns} - \text{capital cost}) \div \text{year of use}}{\text{capital cost}} \times 100$$

The ARR method has several advantages, such as the fact that it shows the profitability of an investment project over a given period of time, allowing comparisons with other investment projects. It has disadvantages too, such as the fact that it does not consider the timing of cash inflows.

HL   The **net present value (NPV)** is the difference between:

- the summation of present values of future cash inflows (returns), calculated using "discount factors" ("discount rates") provided in a "discount table" (in order to convert future cash flows into their present value)

- the original cost of the investment.

$$\text{Net present value (NPV)} = \sum \text{present values of return} - \text{original cost}$$

The NPV method has several advantages, such as the fact that it takes opportunity cost and time value of money into account. It has disadvantages too, such as the fact that it is based on discount rates that may not be well predicted.

QUESTION PRACTICE

S4U is a private limited company that provides a storage facility to households and small businesses. *S4U* is considering constructing an additional new warehouse.

S4U's management has forecasted the following annual net cash flows for the new warehouse:

Year	Net cash flows ($)
0	−150 000
1	25 000
2	30 000
3	35 500
4	37 000
5	39 800
6	41 200

(…)

a) For the new warehouse:

  i) using information from the table above, calculate the average rate of return (ARR) (*show all your working*);   [2]

  ii) using information from the table above, calculate the payback period (*show all your working*);   [2]

iii) using information from the table below, calculate the net present value (NPV) at a discount rate of 6% (*show all your working*). [2]

Years	Discount rate
	6%
1	0.9434
2	0.8900
3	0.8396
4	0.7921
5	0.7473
6	0.7050
7	0.6651
8	0.6271
9	0.5919
10	0.5584

b) Explain **one** disadvantage for *S4U* of using the NPV method of investment appraisal. [2]

>> **Assessment tip**

Questions about investment appraisals are asked often in paper 2 exams so make sure you know how to approach them. Typically, you are given a scenario and you are asked to apply investment appraisal techniques. As they all have advantages and disadvantages, you may be asked to recommend the most suitable one, depending on the scenario and the organization.

SAMPLE STUDENT ANSWER

a) i)

Total returns – capital cost = 208 500 – 150 000 = 58 500

58 500 / 6 = 9750

9750 / 150 000 = 0,065

ARR = 0,065 x 100 = 6,5 %

▲ The result is correct. The candidate duly showed their workings, even though that could be slightly clearer.

This response could have achieved 2/2 marks.

ii)

Year 0	0	
Year 1	25 000	25 000
Year 2	30 000	55 000
Year 3	35 500	90 500
Year 4	37 000	127 500
Year 5	39 800	167 300

Year 4 and x months

39 800 / 12 = 3316 per month

150 000 – 127 500 = 22 500

22 500 / 3316 = 6,7

Payback period = between Year 4 and 6 months and Year 4 and 7 months

▲ The result is correct, even though other methods would have been possible, especially using a formula.

This response could have achieved 2/2 marks.

iii)

Year 1	25 000	0.9434	23 585
Year 2	30 000	0.8900	26 700
Year 3	35 500	0.8396	29 805.8
Year 4	37 000	0.7921	28 119.55
Year 5	39 800	0.7473	29 742.54
Year 6	41 200	0.7050	29 046
TOTAL			166 998.89

166 998.89 rounded up to 167 000

NPV = 167 000 – 150 000 = $17 000

 This is not the correct total. The candidate made an arithmetic error in one of the calculations.

▲ The correct answer is 18 188 so this is not correct; however the candidate clearly understands the principles of NPV, so may score 1 mark.

This response could have achieved 1/2 marks.

b)

The NVP method depends on the choice of the overall discount rate (6% here) and of the national interest rates for each year in the discount. There is no clear reason for the choice of 6%; if they choose another rate, the NVP results will be different.

▲ The answer is concise but clear; the candidate clearly understands one of the disadvantages of the NVP method.

This response could have achieved 2/2 marks.

 Assessment tip

Do not forget the units: payback period in years and months, ARR as a percentage and NPV as an amount of money!

Content link

Link to your IA

Even if your IA is not specifically about finance and accounts, you can apply the contents of this unit to your chosen organization. Do they use investment appraisal methods like the ones covered here?

Content link

Link to other sub-units

- Sub-units 3.8 and 3.7 are linked because there is a close relationship between investment, profit and cash flow.
- Sub-units 3.8 and 5.8 (HL only) are linked because research and development often lead to the decision to invest in a new project, in a new venture.

Concept link

The concept of **sustainability** is very important for investment appraisal. Investing in a new project may be financially worthwhile, ensuring return on investment, but what would be the environmental and socio-cultural impacts? Only considering the financial dimension is not sustainable.

3.9   BUDGETS   HL ONLY

You should be able to:

✔ distinguish between cost centres and profit centres

✔ explain the role of cost centres and profit centres

✔ construct a budget

✔ interpret variances in a budget

✔ analyse the role of budgets and variances in decision making.

This short sub-unit focuses on a quantitative planning tool frequently used by all organizations: budgeting.

Topic summary

Budget

A **budget** is a quantitative financial plan that estimates the revenue and expenditure over a future time period. The **budget holder** is the person responsible for the formulation and achievement of a budget.

Budgets are important for many reasons: they help in planning and setting targets, in allocating resources, in motivating budget holders, in controlling how funds have been spent.

Cost and profit centres

Cost centres are the sections of a business where costs are incurred and recorded, for example by item (wages, electricity, insurance), by department (marketing, production), by project, or by product. **Profit centres** are the sections of a business where both costs and revenues are incurred and recorded, usually by product line, or product. Businesses can then calculate how much profit each centre makes.

Cost centres and profit centres have several roles: they provide information that can aid decision-making, improving accountability, tracking problem areas and benchmarking. Comparison between profit centres is not always easy and could lead to problems such as conflicts or staff stress, as the pressure of managing a budget may be high.

Variances

In budgeting, **variance** is the difference between the budgeted figure and the actual figure. It is calculated at the end of the budget period; it can be "favourable" (when the difference between the budgeted and actual figure is financially beneficial to the firm, for example spending less than anticipated) or "adverse" (when the difference between the budget and actual figure is financially costly to the firm, for example spending more than planned).

Decision making

Budgets and variance analysis play several roles in decision making, especially for strategic planning. They help control revenue and expenditure, setting targets in line with the organization's strategic objectives. They also have limitations, as setting budgets without involving some stakeholders could result in their resentment and affect their motivation levels.

Content link
Link to your IA

Even if your IA is not specifically about finance and accounts, you can apply the contents of this unit to your chosen organization. Do they use budgets? Do they have systems of "cost centres" and "profit centres"? Do they do variance analysis?

 Assessment tip

You could be asked two types of question about budgets:

1   Quantitative questions.

2   Qualitative questions.

Quantitative questions will ask you to calculate something, usually variances:

Complete the variance column in the table below and establish whether the results obtained are adverse (A) or favourable (F).   [6]

$000	Budgeted figure	Actual figure	Variance
Sales revenue	500	420	
Direct labour costs	50	50	
Direct material costs	80	90	
Gross profit	370	280	
Overheads	100	95	
Net profit	270	185	

▲ **Table 1** Budgeted and actual figures for company *ABC Ltd* this year

Qualitative questions will require your answer to be textual, for example:

Define the term "variance analysis".   [2]

Explain the importance of budgets to company *ABC Ltd.*   [4]

Comment on the performance of company *ABC Ltd* using the variance results.   [6]

Content link
Link to other sub-units

- Sub-units 3.9 and 3.7 are linked because budgets and cash flow forecasts have many similarities, although there are some differences, for example budgets do not have an "opening balance" and a "closing balance".

- Sub-units 3.9 and 2.3 are linked because budgeting (creating a budget) and monitoring budgets (analysing variances) are an essential responsibility of managers.

Concept link

The concept of **change** is linked to the topic of budgeting because strategic planning involves deciding how to allocate resources in order to achieve set objectives. Budgets however cannot consider unforeseen changes in the external environment, such as increase in the costs of raw materials, or negative competitive conditions. Budgets therefore should allow for timely revisions, to take these changes into consideration when analysing adverse variance.

4 MARKETING

You should know:

✔ Marketing planning

✔ Sales forecasting (HL only)

✔ Market research

✔ The seven Ps of the marketing mix

✔ International marketing (HL only)

4.1 INTRODUCTION TO MARKETING SOME HL ONLY

You should be able to:

✔ define marketing and its relationship to the other business functions

✔ distinguish between "market orientation" and "product orientation"

✔ calculate and interpret market share and market growth

✔ discuss the importance of market share and market leadership (HL only).

This sub-unit introduces key terms about marketing, one of the four business functions.

Topic summary

Marketing may be defined in many ways: it is about identifying and satisfying customers' needs; it is about getting the right product to the right customers at the right price at the right time.

A **market orientation** starts with market research first, in order to identify a market and its needs; a product will then be conceived and sold to this specific market to respond to a particular demand. This is the foundation of marketing practices. This is the opposite of **product orientation** which focuses first on the product.

A market can be described in different ways:

• By size, either in volume (units) or in value (revenue).

• By growth rate (the percentage change in total market size over a period of time; it can be positive or negative).

Market share is the percentage of one company's share of the total sales in the market:

$$\text{Market share} = \frac{\text{Company's sales}}{\text{Total sales in the market}} \times 100$$

HL | **Market share** can be measured by value (revenue) or volume (units); it is always expressed as a percentage. It makes it possible to identify the **market leader**, the company with the highest market share. Being the market leader has several benefits: the market leader often has "first-mover advantages" in new markets, with

Revision tip

To help you consolidate your learning, you could identify examples of:

- Organizations that have a product orientation. Why is it suitable for them, as opposed to a market orientation?

- Organizations that are market leaders. How did they become market leaders?

an established brand name and the possibility to gain economies of scale. Market leaders need to be careful though, as they could be subject to lawsuits if they become too dominant in certain markets.

QUESTION PRACTICE

In 2010, *ELE* (a fictional business) owned 4.5% of the European Union (EU) car rental market. In 2019, *ELE*'s car rental division had revenues of EUR 0.9 billion in a market worth EUR 16.8 billion. Initially, *ELE* only provided car rentals in its gasoline stations in Belgium. By 2014, *ELE* had expanded the service to its stations in France, Spain and the UK.

(i) Calculate ELE's market share for car rentals in 2019 (*show all your working*). [2]

(ii) Explain **one** reason why *ELE*'s market share has grown. [2]

SAMPLE STUDENT ANSWER

Response 1

▲ The candidate remembered the formula and applied it correctly (i.e. replaced the different elements by the correct numbers for "company sales" and "total market sales").

▼ The calculation is correct but the candidate forgot the percentage sign.

(i) Market share = (sales of the company divided by total market sales) × 100

$$\text{Market share} = \left(\frac{0.9}{16.8}\right) \times 100$$

Market share = 5.35

This response could have achieved 1/2 marks.

▼ The candidate explains market growth, not market share. The answer is partial.

(ii) The market share has grown from 4.5% to 5.35% because they have expanded to other countries, so they offer their car rental services in more places and have more customers. In the Ansoff matrix, this is called "market development" as they offer the same product (car rental) but in new markets (France, Spain and the UK).

This response could have achieved 1/2 marks.

Response 2

▲ The answer is correct and includes the percentage sign.

$$(i) \text{ Market share} = \left(\frac{0.9}{16.8}\right) \times 100$$

Market share = 5.35%

This response could have achieved 2/2 marks.

(ii) ELE market share has grown because they have opened outlets faster than their competitors. Clearly car rental is a very big market (worth almost 17 billion euros) and ELE is only one of the many providers; it is a very competitive business, but as ELE has expanded more than its competitors, their market share has grown in comparison to them.

This response could have achieved 2/2 marks.

▲ The candidate duly explains the increase in market share, with reference to the overall market and to ELE's competitors, showing their understanding of the topic.

Content link
Link to your IA

Even if your IA is not about marketing, you can apply the contents of this sub-unit to your chosen organization. How important is marketing for them? Do they have a product orientation or a market orientation? How would you describe the market where they operate? How would you evaluate their position in this market, compared to their competitors, based on their respective market shares? The organization you chose for your IA gives you the chance to learn more about the contents of this sub-unit in context.

Content link
Link to other sub-units

- This sub-unit introduces unit 4 in general, so all other sub-units 4.2 to 4.6 are linked to it.

- Sub-units 4.1 and 5.2 are linked as the choice of production method may depend on the organization's marketing approach (for example job production rather suits product orientation).

Concept link

The concepts of **ethics** and **change** are important in marketing:

- **Change** because marketers must pay close attention to cultural factors, especially cultural differences (for example in Israel, McDonald's offers kosher burgers, and in India more vegetarian ones) so companies may need to change their offer in different contexts.

- **Ethics** because businesses should consider their ethical responsibilities to promote their products accurately, to protect their customers and to take their wellbeing into account. (For example, how ethical is it to market products that may damage people's health?)

4.2 MARKETING PLANNING

You should be able to:

✔ explain the role of marketing planning

✔ explain the principles of market segmentation to reach a target market

✔ construct and interpret a position map

✔ distinguish between niche market and mass market

✔ explain the importance of having a unique selling point/proposition (USP)

✔ discuss how organizations can differentiate themselves and their products from competitors.

This sub-unit introduces key terms and ideas about marketing such as the importance of marketing planning, and strategies of differentiation from competitors.

Topic summary

A **marketing plan** is a detailed document which includes marketing objectives and marketing strategies, as well as marketing activities (for example promotional campaigns) and the budget allocated to them. **Marketing planning** is the process of setting marketing objectives and devising strategies and tactics to meet these objectives. It has several advantages; for example sharing the marketing plan with other departments and ensuring that the whole organization knows those marketing objectives. Marketing plans can however be rapidly outdated.

Market segmentation is the process of dividing a market into small groups, called **market segments**: sub-groups of consumers with similar characteristics. Markets can be segmented in different ways, using factors such as demographics (age, gender, religion, family characteristics, sexual orientation), geography (country, region, rural/ urban) or psychographics (social and economic status, values).

Market segmentation helps businesses to identify the **target markets** they want to sell to, and to differentiate products and marketing activities according to these target markets. A **niche market** is a small and narrow market segment, whereas a **mass market** is a large, broad market segment. **Niche marketing** (also called concentrated marketing) is a strategy that only targets a specific niche market, whereas mass marketing (also called undifferentiated marketing) targets the entire market.

Product positioning is the analysis of how consumers perceive a product, compared to its competitors. It is usually represented with a diagram called a **position map** (or **perception map**) where the vertical and horizontal axes represent two variables, usually price and quality. Position maps are also useful to help identify gaps or opportunities in the market.

The **USP** (unique selling point, unique selling proposition) is what differentiates a product. Having a USP is essential to get **competitive advantage** and to ensure consumer loyalty.

Organizations can differentiate themselves from their competitors in different ways:

- Product differentiation (very common, with features such as durability, performance or reliability, though competitors can copy or even improve the product)

- Service differentiation (customer service, delivery, installation, after sales service)

- Price differentiation (charging different customer segments different prices for the same product or service)

- Distribution differentiation (focusing on channels of distribution such as retailers)

- Relationship differentiation (focusing on the personal relationships between the organization's staff and the customers)

- Image/reputation differentiation (difficult for new entrants i.e. businesses entering a new market).

QUESTION PRACTICE

Sam is a young entrepreneur. He wants to set up a retail store (AFA) selling fair trade chocolate, but he has insufficient funds. He has written a marketing plan for a local bank manager who is offering young entrepreneurs the chance to seek business finance and advice.

Describe **two** elements of a marketing plan for AFA.   [4]

Response 1

Sam created a marketing plan for a local bank manager who was offering young entrepreneurs the chance to seek business finance and advice. In this the two elements of marketing plan are the finance and advice, in which the finance could be the way in which Sam will confront the problems of a business in the financial part.

> ▼ Finance is not applied to marketing: the candidate does not describe what this means in a marketing plan.

Also the advice, the enthusiasm he has to set up a retail store, the ideas he has in which he wants to put a business to sell chocolates.

> ▼ "Advice" and "enthusiasm" are not elements of a marketing plan. The candidate may be thinking about entrepreneurship and the business idea; this might be relevant for a business plan, but not for a marketing plan.

Note: Only the idea of "finance" can be credited here.

This response could have achieved 1/4 marks.

Response 2

Place: AFA sells its products at pop-up stalls which are temporary retail venues. So, actually Sam doesn't have enough funds, therefore use them can be a good idea because pop-up businesses are flexible and agile.

> ▼ The candidate refers to the marketing mix, with "place" and "price". It is true that the marketing mix may be included in a marketing plan, but in this answer, the two terms "place" and "price" are not well described.

Price: AFA doesn't have enough funds, so Sam could add a little mark up for balance his economy and sustain the business.

This response could have achieved 1/4 marks.

Response 3

One element of a marketing plan would be the marketing budget of the company. As can be seen from the case study, Sam had insufficient funds, hence planning the marketing budget of the company would allow for them to find out how much the company needs for advertisements and thus plan out the costs for the business.

> ▲ Budget is a correct answer: the marketing plan must include a budget, and the candidate explains that it is necessary to have a budget to cover the costs of advertising.

A second element of a marketing plan would be the objectives and strategies of the company. As can be seen from the case study, the marketing plan is for a local bank manager offering young entrepreneurs the chance to seek business finance and advice, hence the presence of the objectives and strategies of the company allows them to attract and motivate more young entrepreneurs as the young entrepreneurs would be able to learn more about the business.

> ▼ Objectives is a correct answer. However the candidate does not refer to the marketing objectives of the company; the answer seems to be rather about a business plan in general, not a marketing plan focusing on marketing Moreover, the text is largely copied from the stimulus material, with little added value.

The questions about marketing are often the ones where many candidates underperform, because marketing may wrongly seem very easy. Candidates have a tendency to write "common sense" answers; they forget that marketing is an academic subject with a technical vocabulary that they should use in exam answers (for example about target market, USP and differentiation).

▲ The characteristic is well described. It is good to see how the candidate uses marketing terminology for example "consumer profile" and "mass market".

Note: The answer is satisfactory. The first element is well described, with a reference to the budget for the advertising, but the second element about objectives is too generic, and not sufficiently about marketing.

This response could have achieved 3/4 marks.

QUESTION PRACTICE

Describe **one** characteristic of a niche market.   [2]

Note: Niche markets can be defined as being small and narrow – but writing such a short definition is not enough to achieve two marks. The question asks you to describe one characteristic; the command term "describe" means give a detailed account. To be detailed enough to achieve two marks, your answer must be longer, for example:

SAMPLE STUDENT ANSWER

A characteristic of a niche market is its very small size. A niche market is well defined and differentiated. It is small and narrow and the consumers have specific needs and wants. They share many features in their consumer profile, within the larger "mass market" of all consumers.

This response could have achieved 2/2 marks.

QUESTION PRACTICE

Davenport Electronics (DE)

Davenport Electronics (DE) is a small company that manufactures remote control electronic devices that open garage doors. The devices are kept in owners' cars. For years, *DE* devices operated in a fashion similar to those of its three competitors.

The three competitors are all larger than *DE*.

	Price of remote control	Quality perception
Company A	High	Medium
Company B	Medium	Medium
Company C	Low	Medium
DE	Medium	High

Using the table, construct a product position map/perception map for all four companies.   [4]

SAMPLE STUDENT ANSWER

▲ The position map is correctly labelled and the four companies are correctly placed. The axes could have been presented differently (quality vertical and price horizontal).

High price

A

Low quality ←——————→ High quality

B   *DE*

C

Low price

This response could have achieved 4/4 marks.

>> **Assessment tip**

If you are asked to construct a position map, you do not need to write any text: just draw the diagram but remember to label the axes; in this case, the horizontal one (*x*-axis) is quality, and the vertical one (*y*-axis) is price. These are the most common labels, but in other cases, it could be cost, budget, efficiency, style etc.

Content link
Link to your IA

Even if your IA is not about marketing, you can apply the contents of this sub-unit to your chosen organization. What are their main targets? Could you draw a perception map for one of their main products? Do they have a USP? How do they differentiate themselves from their competitors?

Content link
Link to other sub-units

- Sub-units 4.2 and 1.3 are closely linked because 1.3 introduces terms such as "strategic objectives" and "tactics" which are also relevant for marketing.

- Sub-units 4.2 and 4.5 are closely linked because 4.5 further explains key elements of marketing, such as product and price, and goes into more detail.

Concept link

The concept of **change** is linked to the topic of marketing planning because marketing planning is not only about short-term decisions (for example about decorating a shop window to attract passing trade into the shop) but also about longer-term objectives (for example about setting objectives such as increasing sales by 5% over the next 3 months). Marketing directors must keep abreast of their customers' changing needs and preferences, and of what their competitors are doing.

4.3   SALES FORECASTING   HL ONLY

You should be able to:

✔ define sales forecasting

✔ explain the terminology of sales forecasting (for example time series analysis)

✔ discuss the benefits and limitations of sales forecasting.

This short sub-unit presents quantitative methods to identify trends in sales and to predict future sales.

HL   **Topic summary**

Sales forecasting is the process of predicting the future sales of a product. It is important for several reasons. It aids the management of stock and cash flow, it helps make informed marketing decisions about pricing and promotion.

Time series analysis is a quantitative sales forecasting method that predicts future sales levels from past sales levels, identifying trends, patterns and variations. These variations can be:

- **Seasonal** – regular changes in demand at different times of the year (for example with a peak before Christmas).

- **Cyclical** – linked to the business cycle in the country's economy (for example with a recession).

- **Random** – unpredictable changes as anomalies in the time series (for example a very mild winter resulting in unusual demand for ice cream).

Calculating **moving averages** is a sales forecasting method that identifies and emphasizes the direction of a trend; it helps smooth out fluctuations from sales data by mapping trends over several years. It is then possible to extrapolate, i.e. to extend the trend line to predict future sales.

Calculating a three-year moving average simply means calculating the mean sales over groups of three years (e.g. 2013–2014–2015, 2014–2015–2016, 2015–2016–2017) and plotting the results on a chart.

Variations are the difference between actual sales and the trend values.

Sales forecasting helps marketing planning and workforce planning, but it has several limitations, especially the fact that it ignores external factors, such as changes in consumer tastes and preferences. It cannot take into account competitors' marketing actions, nor the arrival of new competitors in the market (new entrants). It is also time-consuming because of its complex nature, when considering the calculation of average seasonal variations in each quarter over a number of years.

> **» Assessment tip**
>
> Calculating moving averages and variations is not required in the exam. However, it is important to understand how it is done, and why.

 Content link

Link to other sub-units

Sub-units 4.3 and 3.7 are linked because cash flow forecasts are based on sales forecasts.

 Content link

Link to your IA

Even if your IA is not about marketing, you can apply the contents of this unit to your chosen organization. Do they have seasonal, cyclical or random variations? Do they use tools and techniques to forecast sales? If they do, can you assess the impact of forecast sales and variations from the trend on issues such as resources, costs and planning?

Concept link

The concept of **change** is closely linked to the topic of sales forecasting, because sales forecasting is always affected by changes – some predictable, some not. For some small businesses, it can be a major problem, for example a baker needs to forecast as precisely as possible how many loaves of fresh bread will be sold the next day: if he bakes too many, it will be a waste of resources, but if he bakes too few, some customers will be disappointed.

4.4 MARKET RESEARCH

You should be able to:

✔ discuss why and how organizations carry out market research

✔ explain the main methods of primary market research and the main methods of secondary market research

✔ distinguish between qualitative and quantitative research and between different methods of sampling.

This sub-unit presents the forms, methods and sources of market research.

Topic summary

Market research is the process of collecting, analysing and reporting data related to a particular market. It has several purposes: it can help identify consumers' needs and wants, it can help measure customers' satisfaction and perception of a product, and it also enables organizations to make well-informed marketing decisions.

Market research can be carried out:

- through **primary research** (also called "field research") to collect first-hand information, using the following methods: surveys (through questionnaires), interviews, focus groups, observations

- through **secondary research** (also called "desk research") to collect data that already exists, using the following methods: market analyses (market intelligence reports by special market research agencies), academic journals (scholarly articles written by experts), government publications, media articles and online content.

▼ Table 4.4.1 The differences between **quantitative** and **qualitative** research

Quantitative research	Qualitative research
Collection of numerical data.	Collection of data about opinions, attitudes and beliefs.
Typical method: survey with closed questions.	Typical method: survey with open questions, interviews, focus groups.
Aims to find out "how many?"	Aims to find out "why?"
Objective.	Subjective.
Concise and narrow focus.	Broad and complex focus.

Sampling is the process of selecting a group of people to represent the entire group of customers; this group is called "a sample of the population". The following three sampling techniques are used in marketing (among others that are not part of the DP curriculum, such as "snowball sampling" and "cluster sampling"):

1. Quota sampling, with targets based on proportions.

2. Random sampling, with each person having an equal chance of being chosen.

3. Convenience sampling (also called "opportunity sampling") based on easy access and proximity to the researcher.

>> Revision tip

You must be able to explain the main advantages and disadvantages of the three sampling methods. The following table outlines one advantage and one disadvantage of each:

Sampling method	One advantage	One disadvantage
Quota sampling	Findings are usually quite reliable because the sample is representative of all strata of the population.	The interviewer may be biased in the selection of who is interviewed.
Random sampling	Less bias, as everybody has an equal chance of being chosen.	May not be representative.
Convenience sampling	Easy to do.	Potential for bias and not representative.

>> Revision tip

You must be able to explain the main advantages and disadvantages of all the methods of market research. The following tables outline one advantage and one disadvantage of each:

Primary market research

Method	One advantage	One disadvantage
Survey	Can collect large amount of data rapidly.	The respondents may not understand some of the questions and provide inaccurate answers.
Interview	Can achieve a high response rate.	Time consuming and costly.
Focus groups	Some participants may actively engage because of the interactions with others.	Some members may dominate or influence the group.
Observation	The researcher can see how people behave in a given situation.	Should not be used alone as it only provides partial information.

Secondary market research

Method	One advantage	One disadvantage
Academic journal	Reliable because of the peer-review process.	So specialized that they may not always help for commercial market research.
Media articles and online content	Easily available.	May be too biased to have value.
Government publications	Usually trustworthy statistics and large-scale data about demographics.	May not be up to date.
Market analyses	Detailed and high-quality reports.	Usually expensive.

Secco Vineyards (*SV*) is a family-owned business producing wine in Sonoma, California. They mainly sell in local grocery stores where the competition is intense, so the manager has decided to conduct secondary market research about other possible markets in the US.

With reference to *SV*, explain **one** advantage **and one** disadvantage of using secondary market research. [4]

SAMPLE STUDENT ANSWER

Response 1

> One advantage of secondary research is that SV doesn't have to do any physical work on their own. One disadvantage is that the research may not be very accurate, or it may not contain the information needed to make a business decision.

This response could have achieved 2/4 marks.

▼ The candidate seemingly knows what "secondary market research" is, but the answer is too limited. The first sentence (about the advantage) seems to refer to "desk research" but the statement "doesn't have to do any physical work" is vague, even if the examiner can guess that it means no collection of primary data. The second sentence shows some basic understanding of the disadvantages of secondary research (lack of accuracy, information not useful); however this is not applied to the case study.

Response 2

> One advantage of using secondary market research is that it is very cost-effective. Secondary research is often free, and when it is not, it can be less expensive than the process of doing primary research. As SV is looking for other possible markets in the US, it would be very expensive and time-consuming to do research from Florida to Alaska and from Minnesota to Tennessee. For secondary research, Joe Secco only needs to read about wine consumption in different States.
>
> One disadvantage of using secondary market research is that the information that Joe finds may not be directly useful and relevant for him – for example it may have been collected for a campaign to reduce alcohol consumption, so the conclusions may not be useful for him. Sources of secondary market research can be biased and subjective, so Joe must be careful as he wants to sell alcohol and this can be controversial.

▲ The advantage is clearly explained, with reference to the case study.

▲ The disadvantage is clearly explained, with reference to the case study.

This response could have achieved 4/4 marks.

To know more about his customers, Jacob wanted to carry out primary research; he decided to use the method of convenience sampling.

Explain **one** advantage **and one** disadvantage for Jacob of using convenience sampling. [4]

The advantage is correct but not sufficiently applied; the candidate should have explained that convenience sampling means that Jacob knows the people he samples, which is why they are less likely to refuse to answer.

 The disadvantage is well explained and applied at the very end of the answer.

SAMPLE STUDENT ANSWER

An advantage is that the people he chooses in this convenience sampling method will be less likely to refuse to answer his questions than other people would. A disadvantage is that the results obtained from his research may be biased as his friends and relatives probably not only share backgrounds and opinions (we tend to be close with people who share our worldview), but would also probably share fewer negative opinions as they care about Jacob.

Note: 1 mark for the partial answer about the advantage. 2 marks for the good answer about the disadvantage.

This response could have achieved 3/4 marks.

Content link

Link to your IA

Even if your IA is not about marketing, you can apply the contents of this sub-unit to your IA in two ways:

- How did you collect the data for your IA? Which methods of primary and/or secondary research did you use, and why?
- Does your chosen organization engage in market research? In which forms: using primary and/or secondary methods?

Content link

Link to other sub-units

Sub-units 4.4 and 4.1 are closely linked because market orientation often involves market research in order to understand customers' needs and wants.

Concept link

Ethics plays an important role in marketing research, especially with risks of invasion of privacy, breaches of confidentiality and deceptive practices. In many countries, the legislation around marketing research is becoming tighter and stricter. Participants are often asked to give their informed consent. Their rights must be respected, including the right to withdraw their consent at any point during the research process. They must also be informed if they are being filmed or recorded. Data collection methods must ensure accuracy, reliability, integrity and objectivity. The results must not be manipulated and falsified.

4.5 THE SEVEN Ps OF THE MARKETING MIX SOME HL ONLY

You should be able to:

About product:

✔ explain the stages in a product life cycle

✔ examine various extension strategies that could be used by firms

✔ analyse the relationship between the product life cycle, product portfolio and the marketing mix

✔ comment on the relationship between the product life cycle, investment, profit and cash flow

✔ explain the main aspects of branding (such as brand loyalty)

✔ comment on the importance of branding.

About price:

✔ define the different pricing methods, such as penetration pricing and premium pricing

✔ justify the appropriateness of using different pricing methods

About promotion:

✔ explain the main forms of promotion (such as above the line promotion and below the line promotion)

✔ discuss the role of social media marketing as a promotional strategy.

About place:

✔ examine the importance of different types of distribution channel.

About people:

✔ discuss the importance of employee–customer relationships in marketing a service and cultural variation in these relationships.

About process:

✔ evaluate the importance of delivery processes in marketing a service and changes in these processes.

About physical evidence:

✔ examine the importance of tangible physical evidence in marketing a service.

About the marketing mix as a whole:

✔ evaluate the appropriate marketing mixes for particular products or businesses.

This sub-unit focuses on the seven Ps of the 'marketing mix': product, price, promotion, place, people, process and physical evidence.

Topic summary

Product

The **product life cycle** model shows the five stages that a product goes through, from its introduction to the market:

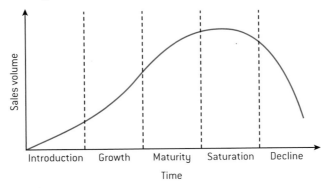

▲ **Figure 4.5.1** The product life cycle model

The product life cycle is closely linked to the marketing mix because different marketing actions will take place at different stages. For example, informative advertising is more necessary in the introduction phase, and pricing strategies may change over time. The product life cycle is also linked to investment, profit and cash flow. For example, investing in promotion is needed in the introductory phase, when there is no profit and the cash flow is negative, whereas in the maturity phase investment is much lower, profit reaches its peak and the cash flow is positive.

Extension strategies are implemented at the maturity or saturation stages in order to avoid decline. The main extension strategies are market development, new packaging and new promotional strategies.

A **brand** is a name, symbol, sign or design that differentiates the products of one company from its competitors. Branding is very important because it has a strong influence on customer perception. The main aspects of branding are **brand awareness** (the ability of consumers to recognize the existence and availability of a company's product), **brand development** (to improve or strengthen the image of a product in the market, for example through promotional campaigns), **brand loyalty** (when consumers become committed to a brand and buy this brand repeatedly) and **brand value** (how much a brand is worth in terms of reputation and potential income).

Packaging plays several roles: it protects the product, it aids branding, it provides information in the contents and can add to the security (for example with anti-theft tabs).

Price

Price is the element of the marketing mix that generates revenue for the business.

The main pricing strategies are:

- **Cost-plus** pricing, easy to calculate by adding a 'mark-up' to the cost of producing a product (for example a percentage)

- **Penetration** pricing, with a low initial price to enter a market or launch a new product (i.e. it is cheaper at first in order to attract buyers)

- **Loss leader** pricing, charging a low price for one product to attract consumers to buy other higher-priced ones
- **Predatory** pricing, charging very low prices in order to drive out competitors (this is illegal in some countries as it is anti-competitive)
- **Premium** pricing, setting a very high price in order to give an impression of exceptional quality or exclusivity (luxury brands do this).

HL HL students are also expected to know the following:

Dynamic pricing, charging different prices depending on who the customers are, or when the products are bought (many airlines do this)

Competitive pricing, setting prices solely according to competitors' prices

Contribution pricing, calculating the variable cost of production in order to set the price

Price elasticity of demand (PED), not a pricing strategy, but a measurement of how the quantity demanded is affected by changes in its price. (If a market is elastic, a small change in price will result in a large change in the quantity demanded; if a market is not elastic, changes in price do not have much impact on customers.) The strategy of **price discrimination** is based on the notion of PED.

HL ## People

People refers to the employees, especially the customer-fronting ones who are the face of the organization, for example the receptionist of a hotel. Interactions with staff constitute the most important element of any service business, as they form a transactional link between the organization and its customers. As part of CRM (Customer Relationship Management), staff are trained to deliver good customer service, whilst taking into account cultural variations and behavioural expectations.

Process

Process refers to the procedures and policies to ensure access to the service, for example the online reservation system for a hotel. Delivery processes are very important in marketing services and businesses keep implementing changes to ensure customer satisfaction and customer loyalty, for example providing easy and varied payment methods, such as paying online payment, ensuring after-sales services or speeding up delivery. This is particularly important for e-commerce.

Physical evidence

Physical evidence refers to the visible aspects that the customer will encounter, for example the cleanliness and style of the lobby and bedroom of a hotel. The intangible nature of services makes it difficult for consumers to evaluate the service being offered before deciding to buy, so the appearance of the physical evidence is an important marketing element.

>> **Assessment tip**

There are often exam questions about the contents of this long unit, so make sure you revise it well. It is a very important one.

Appropriate marketing mixes

The marketing mix is a system: its seven elements are interdependent. An appropriate marketing mix must be coherent, with 7Ps that complement each other logically, to target the right customers. An appropriate marketing mix ensures that consumers' needs and wants are met by producing the right product at the right price, available at the right place and communicated through the right promotion channels. In addition to hiring the right people, this involves adopting efficient procedures and paying attention to any visible touch points that are observable to customers.

Promotion

The aim of promotion is to obtain new customers or retain existing ones ("returning customers") by communicating information about the product. This can be done through:

- **above the line promotion**, paying for advertising in independent mass media such as television, radio or newspapers

- **below the line promotion**, through direct mail, trade shows, public relations and sales promotion; this is cheaper and more focused

- **through the line promotion**, combining above the line and below the line promotion strategies.

Social media marketing (SMM) is a marketing approach that uses social networking platforms to market a firm's products, i.e. word-of-mouth promotion powered by technology through traffic on social media sites (such as Instagram, LinkedIn, Facebook, Twitter, etc). SMM has advantages such as its wide reach and cost savings, but also some disadvantages such as accessibility problems.

Place

Place is about how the product reaches its customers, i.e. **distribution channels**, ranging from zero intermediary (direct: producer to consumer) to several intermediaries (such as agents, wholesalers, retailers).

Product, price, place and promotion are the four elements of the "marketing mix" of goods (i.e. tangible products). This model is often called "the four Ps". The marketing of services require three other elements: people, process and physical evidence. As they also start with the letter P, this model of the "extended marketing mix" is called "the seven Ps".

>> **Assessment tip**

"Place" does not mean location in a geographical sense: it is about distribution. This is the most common mistake made by students in exam answers about the marketing mix.

QUESTION PRACTICE

Utopia is a luxury holiday resort. It relies heavily on word of mouth for promotion and it has a very strong brand.

With reference to *Utopia*, explain two benefits of having a strong brand.   [4]

SAMPLE STUDENT ANSWER

Examining Utopia's performance over time, it is without a doubt that they have achieved and effectively developed a strong brand. This refers to branding which is what differentiates Utopia from any other competitor in the market. In summary it is what makes a business unique and valuable for a target market. With Utopia achieving a strong brand, this would increase sales and profits in the long run, thus entailing an extended customer base, and therefore achieving customer loyalty. Also, obtaining a strong brand allows Utopia to make efficient use of their working capital to furthermore improve the brand in various aspects, along with coming up with new ideas such as the 3D printer to produce customized souvenirs in order to develop Utopia's offering of exceptional services to its customers; whether existing or potential.

▲ The answer starts with a definition of branding; this is not necessary and it does not result in any extra marks, but it shows that the candidate understands the topic of branding.

▲ The first benefit is well explained, linking an increase in sales and profit with brand loyalty.

▼ The second benefit links strong brand with working capital and investment, though it is less clear, especially in terms of continuously improving the brand: how is this a benefit? This could be better explained.

Note: The answer is clear overall, using the case study, though the second benefit could be better explained, for a higher score.

This response could have achieved 3/4 marks.

QUESTION PRACTICE

AFA is a business selling fair trade products (chocolate, coffee, clothing and stationery) in pop-up stalls and maybe online soon too.

With reference to *AFA*, explain the importance of branding.   [6]

SAMPLE STUDENT ANSWER

Branding is crucial to AFA as it helps to improve AFA's sales revenue through increased sales. It is important for AFA to develop a good brand image, to raise brand awareness so as to attract customers. Branding proved to be important to AFA, as their mission to supply fair trade products "was proving to be very popular with his customers". Customers recognized the mission of AFA and would help AFA to generate larger revenue stream and possibly profit margins with more sales.

▲ The candidate correctly uses terms about the importance of branding, such as "brand awareness".

▲ The occasional use of quotations from the case study helps ensure that the answer is not only theoretical, but linked to the case study.

▲ The candidate correctly uses business management in their answer, for example discussing "revenue stream" and "profit margins"; this shows that the candidate is not only knowledgeable about marketing, but about other parts of the subject too.

▲ The answer shows that the candidate knows about several roles and goals of branding.

▲ The candidate makes good links between different elements of the course, for example considering several stakeholders.

▲ The final part of the answer adds an original and less common idea about the importance of branding for one more stakeholder: employees. The candidate explains why some employees may be attracted to work for this company because of their brand and what it represents.

Branding is also important at establishing the position in the market. Given that "AFA was a great success" and "sales revenue had grown significantly", it was likely that AFA had a large market share. This would be beneficial to AFA as it could give them advantages such as attracting suppliers and banks who would want to support AFA and gives AFA better bargaining power because of its strong brand presence. Thus, branding is important.

Branding is also important in attracting employees who share the same ideals and goals as AFA. AFA has branded itself as a business that is "fully dedicated to fair trade products", and Sam's focus on corporate social responsibility would brand the business in an ethical way, helping to attract employees who share the same vision as Sam. Thus, branding is important.

Note: This long answer is clear and well structured; it is particularly good to see how each paragraph presents an argument, with examples, and ends with a conclusion summarizing the answer. This helps ensure that the whole text stays focused and does not go off course, for example about other aspects of marketing.

This response could have achieved 6/6 marks.

QUESTION PRACTICE

Secco Vineyards (SV) is a family-owned business producing wine in Sonoma, California. Using cost-plus (mark-up) pricing, they sell their wine in local grocery stores. Competition is intense, so the managers are considering adopting other pricing strategies.

Given the intense competition, explain **two** pricing strategies SV might consider. [4]

SAMPLE STUDENT ANSWER

Response 1

▼ Mark-up pricing is a pricing strategy that SV could consider, but the candidate does not explain why. The other answer (odd-even pricing) is not credited.

Two pricing strategies that Secco Vineyards might consider could be odd-even pricing and mark-up pricing.

This response could have achieved 1/4 marks.

Response 2

▲ The first pricing strategy (loss leader) is suitable and well explained in context.

The first pricing strategy they could use is loss leader: it means that they would sell one of their wines at a very low price (for example, one type of white wine) to attract new customers, and then they sell the other wines (for example, red wine) at a higher rate to make up for the loss on the white wine. This can help attract many new customers to SV wines.

The second pricing strategy they could use is competitive pricing (predatory) given the "intense competition" (line 12) taking into account competitors' prices and charging just under.

▼ The second pricing strategy is relevant but it is not clearly explained; in particular, it is not clear how the company, having financial difficulties, could sustain a strategy of predatory pricing.

Note: The first pricing strategy is clear and well explained; the second less so.

This response could have achieved 3/4 marks.

QUESTION PRACTICE

Utopia is a luxury holiday resort. It relies heavily on word of mouth for promotion.

With reference to *Utopia*, explain the role of promotion.   [6]

SAMPLE STUDENT ANSWER

Response 1

The promotion that Utopia currently uses is word of mouth for promotion. This is a kind of below the line promotion which does not use paid-for and mass media as the way to promote its products. Instead, word of mouth promotion relies on people spread out the information and inform other people about the product. Promotion is used to promote and sell its products and services to different existing or potential consumers. Since Utopia offers a unique and once in a lifetime tourist experience, their target consumers are relatively rich like the film stars. By using word of mouth, they may attract other film stars to experience their service. Plus, the viral marketing which spreads information through social network websites and email is a way for people knowing Utopia which reach its goal of promotion.

▼ The candidate answers a different question about promotion, about word of mouth promotion – however this is not the question asked, even though there is the word "promotion".

▲ This sentence starts addressing the question: "promote and sell its products and services".

▼ The final part of the answer is not directly relevant: it is about word of mouth again, and viral marketing.

Note: The candidate wrote about forms of promotion, not about the role of promotion: to create awareness, to inform customers, to persuade them. Little in this short answer is relevant or can be credited.

This response could have achieved 2/6 marks.

Response 2

Promotion is the act of advertising and giving information about a product to customers. The role of promotion at Utopia is extremely important.

▲ The answer starts with a short definition, which is good practice.

▲ The candidate explains a first role of promotion (to attract new customers) with reference to the case study, as required.

First of all, promotion enables Utopia to attract more customers. Currently Utopia's promotion relies heavily on word of mouth. Although word of mouth is not a strong promotion strategy compared to above the line promotion strategies such as TV advertising, it will help Utopia attract new customers. By attracting more customers, Utopia will be able to generate more sales revenue.

▲ The candidate explains a second role of promotion (to build a positive brand image) again with reference to the case study, as required.

Moreover, promotion can also benefit Utopia by building a positive brand image. By promoting Utopia's exceptional once in a lifetime experience, Utopia will be able to build a positive brand image. A positive brand image is especially important for Utopia as it can lead to brand loyalty which would make customers make repeated purchases and this will give Utopia more profit.

Note: The answer is good overall, though it could be more developed, for an even higher mark. Everything written is correct, and the structure is clear, but the examiner would expect a longer answer with other points about the role of promotion.

This response could have achieved 5/6 marks.

🔗 **Content link**
Link to other sub-units

- Sub-units 4.5 and 4.2 are closely linked because 4.2 introduces the wider context of marketing planning: the marketing mix requires careful planning.

- Sub-units 4.5 and 4.4 are closely linked because the marketing mix must be based on marketing research.

🔗 **Content link**
Link to your IA

Even if your IA is not about marketing, you can use and apply the contents of this unit to your chosen organization. You could prepare a full marketing analysis of one of their products, you could examine their promotional mix or their distribution channel, or you could study their pricing strategies.

Concept link

The concepts of **creativity** and **change** are linked to the topic of the marketing mix:

- **Creativity** is required in all aspects of the marketing mix, from product development to packaging (e.g. reducing unnecessary plastic wrapping) to promotion (e.g. harnessing digital technologies such as viral marketing on social media).

- **Change**, because the seven Ps are interrelated within a coherent marketing strategy. Changes in one "P" have an impact on the others, for example starting to sell online and distribute through e-commerce may require changes in the promotion channels, or launching a new product may involve a penetration pricing strategy for that product, which requires clear communication to manage the brand well.

4.6 INTERNATIONAL MARKETING HL ONLY

You should be able to:

✔ analyse how businesses enter international markets

✔ examine the opportunities and threats posed by entry into international markets.

This sub-unit focuses on the marketing of goods and services across national boundaries.

HL

Topic summary

International marketing refers to the marketing of goods and services across national boundaries. There is a difference between global marketing (where firms use a standardized approach to market their products in other countries) and international marketing (where firms adapt their 7 Ps and their marketing approach to suit the culture and expectations of their new customers in different countries). Increasing worldwide competition and **globalization** are the main cause of the rise in international marketing.

The main methods of entry into international markets are:

* **E-commerce**: trading over the internet.

* **Exporting**: directly or indirectly, through an agent or by "piggybacking" (i.e. using the distribution channels of another company already present in the foreign markets).

* **Foreign direct investment**: setting a production plant (factory) in another country (i.e. investing in that country).

* **International joint venture**: setting up a new company in partnership with a local one.

* **International franchising**: granting a franchise to a franchisee in another country.

Entry into international markets provides many opportunities, such as market development, enhanced brand image and economies of scale. It also poses many threats, economically (for example fluctuating exchange rates), politically (as some countries are less stable than others, so doing business there may be problematic), legally (as some countries have protectionist barriers, making it difficult to export there) and linguistically (notably when trading with countries that speak different languages).

>> **Assessment tip**

There are not often questions specifically about international marketing, but you must know and understand the topic, as you may refer to it in your answers to other questions, for example about external growth or market development.

Content link
Link to other sub-units

* Sub-units 4.6 and 1.5 are linked because several external growth methods (such as joint venture and franchising) are also methods of entry into international markets.

* Sub-units 4.6 and 1.6 are linked because MNCs operate in several countries and therefore engage in international marketing.

Content link
Link to your IA

Even if your IA is not about marketing, you can use and apply the contents of this sub-unit to your chosen organization. Do they engage in international marketing? If yes, what opportunities and threats have they encountered?

Concept link

All four concepts help understand the topic of international marketing:

- **Ethics**, because international marketing means trading across national borders, with customers who may have different ethical values, beliefs and attitudes (for example, some promotional material may need to be revised, as it may be seen as unacceptable in the other country, for cultural reasons).

- **Change**, because entry into foreign markets implies many changes in the organization, in all areas, from finance (payment in foreign currencies) to logistics (to ensure distribution in other countries, possibly other continents) and from HR (with the need for translators) to legal affairs (to ensure compliance with national standards and regulations).

- **Creativity,** because some products may need to be modified and adapted for the international market, to suit customers themselves (for example their taste in food), their culture (for example cars with the steering wheel on the right or left side) or to conform to the country's legislation (for example health and safety).

- **Sustainability,** because local supply chains are usually seen as more sustainable, so international marketing is sometimes criticized for its lack of sustainability; marketers may have to show that their practice is sustainable from another perspective, for example generating job opportunities or contributing to local communities.

5 OPERATIONS MANAGEMENT

You should know:

✔ The role of operations management

✔ Operations methods

✔ Lean production and quality management (HL only)

✔ Location

✔ Break-even analysis

✔ Production planning (HL only)

✔ Crisis management and contingency planning (HL only)

✔ Research and development (HL only)

✔ Management information systems (HL only)

5.1 INTRODUCTION TO OPERATIONS MANAGEMENT

You should be able to:

✔ define operations and outline their relationship to other business functions

✔ explain the role of operations management.

This short sub-unit introduces the business function that deals with the production of goods and services: operations management.

Topic summary

Operations are the fundamental activities of all organizations. The term can be defined as "what they do and deliver"; another word for it is "production". The three other business functions support and enable operations:

• Human resources – because operations are done by people.

• Accounts and finance – because operations generate revenue but they need to be properly funded.

• Marketing – because operations produce goods and services that must be promoted, marketed and sold.

>> **Assessment tip**

There are not often questions about operations management in generic terms, but for the paper 1 and paper 3 case studies, it is important:

• that you identify the organization's key operations

• that you identify how these operations are linked to the other business functions.

This will help you to understand the purpose of the organization and recommend possible strategies, for example to increase workforce capabilities, to modify the goods and services produced, or to invest in more equipment.

🔗 **Content link**
Link to your IA

Even if your IA is not about operations management, you can apply the contents of this sub-unit to your chosen organization. What are its key operations? What goods and services are produced – and by whom? What role does operations management play in the organization? The organization you chose for your IA gives you the chance to learn more about the contents of this sub-unit in context.

Content link

Link to other sub-units

- Sub-unit 1.1 is linked to this sub-unit because all businesses, in all sectors, are based on operations.
- Sub-unit 2.1 because human resources are essential to enable operations.
- Sub-unit 3.8 because investment usually enables an improvement or an increase in operations.
- Sub-unit 4.5 because products are created by operations.

Concept link

The concept of **sustainability** is linked to the topic of operations as operations should aim to be sustainable in the economic, social, and environmental domain – following the "triple bottom line" model: Profitability, People and Planet.

5.2   OPERATIONS METHODS

This sub-unit introduces the main methods of production of goods.

You should be able to:

✔ distinguish between the following methods of production:
- ✔ job production
- ✔ batch production
- ✔ mass production
- ✔ mass customization

✔ recommend the most appropriate method of production for a given situation.

Topic summary

There are four methods of production:

- **Job production** (also called "customized production") is the most market-oriented: customers decide exactly what the product should be, for example a personalized birthday cake with your name on it.
- **Batch production** is suitable for identical products, made in groups ("batches"), for example a dozen cakes with the same flavour.
- **Mass production** (also called "flow production" "standardized production" and "process production") creates a high volume of standardized products (for example identical loaves of bread).
- **Mass customization** (sometimes called "mass individualized customization") combines mass production with the personalization of custom-made products. Customers can personalize the goods they order and make them unique.

They each have advantages and disadvantages. Mass production, for example, can achieve economies of scale, unlike job production; however, it is based on the principle of "product orientation" which, in marketing terms, is not always suitable as it is not market-led. Mass customization shares most features of mass production, the main difference being that finished stock cannot be prepared in advance, though it is rapidly finalized.

In each situation, one method may be more appropriate than others, depending on several factors, such as the target market, the state of technology and the availability of resources.

Test yourself

Can you represent each method of production in the form of a diagram or a flow chart? This is not an exam question, but this creative challenge can help you check that you understand the differences between the methods of production.

QUESTION PRACTICE

This question refers to a pastry shop called *EP* that uses mass customization for its celebration desserts and party cakes (for birthdays, quinceañeras etc) as customers like to request special messages to be written on them.

Explain **one** advantage and **one** disadvantage for *EP* of using mass customization for its birthday cakes.   [4]

SAMPLE STUDENT ANSWER

Response 1

The advantage of mass customization is the fact that it combines both mass production and customization.

The disadvantage is the fact they cannot keep a stock of ready-made cakes: they cannot use just-in-case production as the names on the cakes may vary, so they use just-in-time.

This response could have achieved 1/4 marks.

▼ The advantage outlined does not show that the candidate knows what mass customization means: it only breaks down the term into its two components (mass + customization).

▲ The disadvantage outlined is correct, but it is not sufficiently explained. The answer is correct but too short to warrant 2 marks. It should be longer and more developed.

Response 2

The advantage of mass customization for EP is the fact that their clients have the impression that they purchase a cake made just for them, with their name on it, as it is personalized. This is important for customer satisfaction, this is an advantage about marketing and reputation, but is also about finance: repeat customers will choose EP cakes because of the extra touch, it is their USP (unique selling point).

▲ The advantage is well explained in the context of the pastry shop.

The disadvantage is the fact that EP cannot prepare and stock ready-made cakes, so customers must order them in advance for the final personalization. This is not a big disadvantage because customers must know that and cannot expect to just go to the pastry shop and find a cake with their names on it. The main part of the cake is same anyway (and probably was prepared by batch production for different sizes and types and flavours) and only the final stage of production is personalized.

▲ The disadvantage is well explained in the context of the pastry shop.

This response could have achieved 4/4 marks.

Content link
Link to your IA

Even if your IA is not about operations management, you could apply the contents of this sub-unit to your chosen organization if they manufacture goods. What method(s) of production do they use, and why? What are the advantages and the disadvantages?

Content link
Link to other sub-units

- Sub-unit 2.2 about organizational structure is linked to this sub-unit.
- Sub-unit 2.4 about motivation is linked to this sub-unit.

Assessment tip

Command terms are very important: you can always get some points if you show your knowledge of the course contents, but for full marks your answer must do what you are asked to do in the question. To assess that you know the meaning of "mass production", the exam question could be:

1) "Define the term mass production."   [2 marks]

Or

2) "Outline one feature of mass production."   [2 marks]

Concept link

All concepts are linked to the topic of production methods, especially **change** and **creativity**:

- **Change**, because the choice of production methods will change over time, for example if the organization starts to offer highly specialized, one-off products that require job production.
- **Creativity**, because process innovation may result in more efficient techniques: this is how fast food restaurants developed in the twentieth century.

5.3   LEAN PRODUCTION AND QUALITY MANAGEMENT   HL ONLY

This sub-unit examines the features and methods of lean production and the principles of quality management.

You should be able to:

- ✔ define lean production and describe its main features
- ✔ explain the main methods of lean production
- ✔ explain the features of "cradle to cradle" design and manufacturing
- ✔ distinguish between quality control and quality assurance
- ✔ explain the following methods of managing quality:
  - ✔ quality circle
  - ✔ benchmarking
  - ✔ total quality management (TQM)
- ✔ evaluate the impact of lean production and TQM on an organization
- ✔ explain the importance of national and international quality standards.

HL   Topic summary

Operations management is increasingly using principles of **lean production** in order to cut waste, be more efficient, save money and be more sustainable.

Lean production uses several methods including:

- *Kaizen,* a Japanese term that refers to **continuous improvement** and continuous changes at all levels of the organization in order to improve processes.

- **Just-in-time** (JIT) to reduce the stocks of both raw materials and finished products.

Cradle to cradle (C2C) design and manufacturing is a recent model of **sustainability** stating that once a product is used, it should be recycled in order to recreate the same product.

Quality control and quality assurance should ensure that all products are safe, reliable and offer value for money. **Quality control** means inspecting finished products to check that they meet the desired level of quality, whereas **quality assurance** monitors quality standards across the entire production process.

Managing quality can be done in several ways, such as:

- **Quality circles**: groups of volunteers who meet to discuss ways of improving quality.

- **Benchmarking**: comparing products against competitors' products.

- **Total quality management (TQM)**: an approach to improving quality across the organization, combining several quality tools such as quality chains (involving suppliers) and SPC (Statistical Process Control) data.

Lean production and TQM are closely linked; they have many advantages, such as the fact that they can reduce costs (especially in the long term), but also disadvantages, such as the fact that it may take time to change the culture and practices of an organization.

National and international quality standards are increasingly important in all industries. Meeting recognized standards can help businesses that want to export, giving a competitive edge and reassuring potential customers.

QUESTION PRACTICE

Describe **one** method of lean production **other than** recycling.　　[2]　

SAMPLE STUDENT ANSWER

> With lean production being the process of reducing waste to boost overall efficiency and performance of a certain organization, JIT would be a highly appropriate method of lean production. JIT is a stock control system where the business would keep zero or minimum stock in order to improve the efficiency of the working capital, along with the efficiency of stocks themselves. There will be less storage costs, yet Utopia may run out of stock in the case of an unexpected order (demand).

▲ The method of lean production chosen by the candidate is JIT. There were other possible responses such as *kaizen*. The description of JIT is clear and shows full understanding.

This response could have achieved 2/2 marks.

>> **Assessment tip**

Make sure you know precise definitions of all the terms in this sub-unit – as there are often exam questions asking you to define *kaizen*, benchmarking or TQM.

Content link

Link to your IA

Even if your IA is not about operations management, you could apply the contents of this sub-unit to your chosen organization. Do they use principles of lean management, benchmarking or TQM? How do they control the quality of the goods they produce?

Test yourself

Explain the difference between quality control and quality assurance.

Content link

Link to another sub-unit

JIT is further explained in sub-unit 5.6 (HL only), in contrast to another method of stock control called JIC.

Concept link

All concepts are linked to the topic of lean management, especially sustainability.

Lean management was invented in Japan in the 1950s, decades before the concept of **sustainability** (formulated in the 1970s and 1980s) but they share key ideas, for example: not wasting resources, recycling whenever possible and searching for greater efficiency.

5.4   LOCATION

This sub-unit focuses on the reasons for the choice of a location for a business, and on the factors to consider when relocating production.

You should be able to:

✔ analyse the reasons for the choice of location of production

✔ evaluate the following ways of reorganizing production, both nationally and internationally:

    ✔ outsourcing/subcontracting

    ✔ offshoring

    ✔ insourcing

    ✔ reshoring.

Topic summary

One of the most important decisions that a business has to make is where it will locate (or relocate) production. Numerous factors influence the **choice of the location** or **relocation** of a production facility, such as cost (of land, labour and transport), competition, available infrastructure and transport/logistics networks, land, labour pool (human resources nearby), government (and local authorities), proximity to suppliers, familiarity with the area etc.

Outsourcing (subcontracting) is the practice of using another business (as a "third party") to complete some parts of the work ("peripheral activities"); the organization can then focus on its core activity. **Offshoring** is an extension of outsourcing: it means outsourcing to another country ("offshore" = overseas, abroad). **Insourcing** (in-housing) is the opposite: it is the practice of performing peripheral activities internally, for example to be able to control costs or quality. **Reshoring** is the process of bringing these activities back into the home country.

When considering relocating (including offshoring), it is helpful to distinguish between "pull factors" and "push factors". "Pull factors" attract to a particular place or country (for example better infrastructure, proximity to raw materials, access to wider labour pool, tax incentives) whereas "push factors" are reasons to move from current location (for example negative economic climate and increase in energy costs).

QUESTION PRACTICE

This question is about Su, the owner of a business called *Afghan Sun*. For the location of the plant, Su hesitates between two very different locations, in two countries called A and B.

Su is considering two possible locations for the production facility. Explain the factors (reasons) that Su may consider when deciding between the two locations.

[6]

SAMPLE STUDENT ANSWER

Response 1

Location refers to the geographic site of a business.

A factor that Su may consider when deciding between the two is the government assistance that the locations offer. Since Su needs some more financial assistance for Afghan Sun, this may be a very important factor for her to consider. Su may lean more towards location B as location B encourages investments from overseas with grants available. This description fits Afghan Sun perfectly, and through this Su may be able to reduce the cost of production of her main facility further in order to enable a very low price to be charged (line 24). Therefore, Su and her production team may want to consider this external factor to decide between the two locations.

Another factor that Su may consider when deciding between the two locations is the facilities of the two locations. The facilities are important because it will act as the fixed cost of the whole production, no matter how much solar power Su's factory produces, it will not change. Thus it's best to choose a facility with lower rent to keep her costs of production low. For location A, the facilities require new facilities and high rent, Su may not be able to cover the costs of it as she doesn't have a great lot of funds at the moment (250K from table 2).

▲ The first sentence (definition of location) is not necessary but it enables the candidate to focus their mind on the topic of the question and to show the examiner that they know the meaning of "location" in this context.

▲ The first factor (availability of government assistance) is well explained, with reference to the case study. The candidate does not only explain why government assistance is important for Su's company, but also why it can be a factor to help choose between the two countries (location B rather than location A).

▲ The second factor (facilities) is well explained, with reference to the case study. The candidate does not only explain why this factor is important for Su, but also why location A is not suitable, as it would be too expensive regarding facilities (with the need to construct new ones and to pay high rent for them).

Note: The answer is good and clearly structured. The candidate duly explains two factors that both lead to the selection of country B for the location of the production facility.

The question refers to "factors" in the plural; two was the minimum number, which is what the candidate has given.

Content link
Link to your IA

Even if your IA is not about operations management, you could apply the contents of this sub-unit to your chosen organization. Where are they located? Why? What factors made them choose this location? What would be the advantages and disadvantages of a relocation?

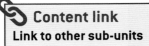
Content link
Link to other sub-units

- Sub-unit 1.6 about multinational companies (MNCs) as many MNCs develop through offshoring.

- Sub-unit 2.2 as changes in organizational structure may be necessary when production location is relocated or outsourced.

The candidate integrates elements from the case study well in the answer, for example about the financial resources available ($250K, see last sentence).

The candidate could have added a conclusion at the end to recap the points made and to state that other factors could/should also be taken into consideration, such as political stability or infrastructure.

This response could have achieved 5/6 marks.

Concept link

All concepts are linked to the topics of location and relocation:

- **Sustainability:** relocating can help a company become more sustainable in the long term (for example moving into a new building with better thermal insulation).

- **Change:** relocating is a major strategic decision that senior managers never take lightly, as it involves numerous changes, not only in terms of geography, but also possibly in terms of legislation, language and culture. Relocating may also affect both the structure and the culture of the organization, with the arrival of new employees.

- **Ethics:** employees may not be able and willing to move to another town or even another country, if their employer relocates.

- **Creativity:** the ecosystem and culture of innovation of a particular city or region may be a factor that leads new start-ups to locate or relocate there, for example Bengaluru in India or Silicon Valley in the USA.

5.5   BREAK-EVEN ANALYSIS

This sub-unit focuses on break-even analysis, an important tool that helps a company calculate and see at what point it starts making profit.

You should be able to:

✔ distinguish between "contribution per unit" and "total contribution"

✔ construct a break-even chart with the break-even quantity/point (BEQ/BEP)

✔ calculate the break-even quantity, profit (or loss), margin of safety, target profit output, target profit and target price

✔ explain the effects of changes in price or cost on the break-even analysis, profit and margin of safety, using graphical and quantitative methods

✔ discuss the benefits and limitations of break-even analysis.

Topic summary

The **contribution** shows how much a product contributes to the fixed costs and thus to the overall profit of a business, after deducting the variable costs:

(1)   **Contribution per unit = price per unit – variable cost per unit**

The contribution per unit is needed to calculate the break-even point.

(2)   **Total contribution = total revenue – total variable costs**

Total contribution can also be calculated with this formula:

Total contribution = contribution per unit × number of units sold

After establishing the total contribution, profit can then be calculated:

Profit = total contribution – total fixed costs

Profit = (contribution per unit × number of units sold) – total fixed costs

Which corresponds to:

Profit = total revenue – total variable costs – total fixed costs

Profit = total revenue – total costs

The **break-even quantity** (BEQ) is the minimum number that must be sold so that all costs are covered by revenues. At the **break-even point**, (BEP) there is no loss, but no profit either.

They can be calculated **numerically or graphically** on a **break-even chart**.

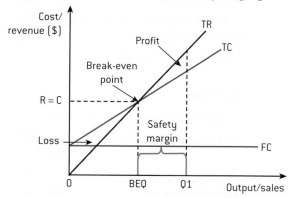

▲ Figure 5.5.1 A break-even chart with margin of safety

The break-even quantity can be calculated in two ways:

1. Using the "contribution per unit" method:

$$\text{Break-even quantity} = \frac{\text{Fixed costs}}{\text{Contribution per unit}}$$

2. Using the "total costs = total revenue" method.

Once the break-even point is reached, it is said that the company is "breaking even" – and it then starts making profit.

Before the BEP, it is a situation of loss. It is then possible to calculate the **margin of safety** i.e. the output amount that exceeds the break-even quantity, using the following formula:

Margin of safety = current output – break-even output

Based on the break-even quantity formula, two other calculations are possible:

$$\text{Target profit output} = \frac{\text{Fixed costs + target profit}}{\text{Contribution per unit}}$$

$$\text{Break-even revenue} = \frac{\text{Fixed costs}}{\text{Contribution per unit}} \times \text{price per unit}$$

>> Revision tip

Questions about break-even are asked frequently in paper 2, so make sure you know how to answer questions about break-even. There is an element of mathematics because business management has a quantitative dimension, which is why paper 2 is mainly quantitative.

On the break-even chart, it is possible to observe the effect of changes in price and in costs, especially how an increase in fixed costs or in variable costs pushes the break-even quantity higher, with a decrease in the margin of safety.

Break-even analysis has several advantages (for example: the chart is easy to use and interpret) but also disadvantages (for example: it assumes that all costs and revenues are linear, which is not always the case, for example with price reductions or discounts).

QUESTION PRACTICE

Moverse

Moverse operates in the health and fitness sector. *Moverse* is not a traditional gym with machines (equipment) and fitness instructors (trainers). The instructors themselves travel and run fitness classes in the buildings of large companies. Instructors all work part-time and are paid wages on a time rate basis.

Moverse currently sells its services to several large companies. They have a total of 727 employees enrolled on its programme.

- *Moverse* charges a yearly fee of $145 for each employee participating.

- *Moverse's* fixed costs are $60 000 per year.

- The variable cost per employee taking part in the programme is $45.

a) Calculate the break-even quantity for *Moverse* (*show all your working*). [2]

b) Construct a fully labelled break-even chart, to scale, for *Moverse* if 800 employees enrol on *Moverse's* training programme. [4]

c) Calculate the profit or loss if 800 employees enrol on *Moverse's* training programme (*show all your working*). [2]

SAMPLE STUDENT ANSWER

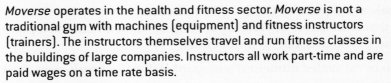

a) Break-even quantity = 60 000/145−45 = 600

BEQ = 600 employees

This response could have achieved 2/2 marks.

▲ The break-even quantity is calculated by dividing the total of fixed costs ($60 000) by the contribution per unit (selling price of $145 per employee participating minus $45 variable cost per employee participating). The candidate recalls and applies the formula well.

≫ Assessment tip

When you read such a stimulus, the main difficulty is to identify different elements. In order to calculate the contribution per unit, ask yourself "what is the unit?" In this case, the unit is the employee taking part in the fitness programme, hence the final answer written: the BEQ (break-even quantity) is 600 "employees" as "units".

b)

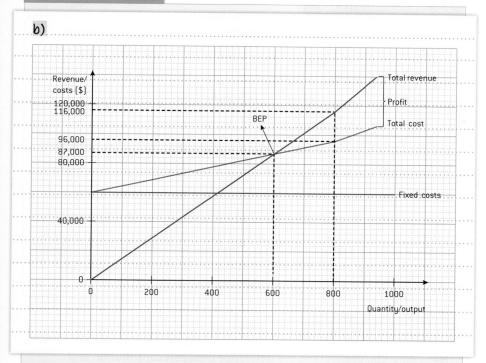

Note: All the aspects assessed are correct:

- The chart is fully labelled.
- All the lines are accurately drawn.
- The break-even point is correctly placed.

This response could have achieved 4/4 marks.

>> **Assessment tip**

Do not forget to label the break-even chart fully, with the axes and lines.
Some marks are always awarded for this; these marks are easy to achieve,
but they are also easy to miss out on, if you forget to add the labels and
the names of the different elements.

c) Total revenue = 800 × 145 = 116 000

Total costs = 60 000 + (800 × 45) = 96 000

Profit = total revenue − total cost = 116 000 − 96 000

= 20 000

Profit = $20 000

▲ The answer is correct and the
candidate showed their workings
(i.e. they did not just write the final
answer ($20 000)).

This response could have achieved 2/2 marks.

>> Assessment tip

There are two ways to calculate profit. The candidate used the formula:

Profit = total revenue – total variable costs – total fixed costs

The alternative was to use the formula:

Profit = total contribution – total fixed costs

i.e.

Profit = (contribution per unit × number of units sold) – total fixed costs

So in this case:

Contribution per unit = 145 – 45 = $100

Profit = (100 × 800) – 60 000 = 80 000 – 60 000 = $20 000

It does not matter which method you choose. Once you have obtained your result, it is worth spending a couple of minutes to double check your result, using the other method. You will be reassured if both answers match, or you will be able to spot that you made a mistake and then correct it.

>> Assessment tip

Make sure you understand the difference between **contribution** and **profit**, as some candidates mix them up:

- Contribution is the difference between the sales prices and the variable costs of a product; this then contributes to the fixed costs and goes towards the profit of the business.
- Profit is the difference between sales and all costs (both variable costs and fixed costs). It is the total revenue minus all the costs. If the costs are higher than the sales revenue, the result is "a negative profit", i.e. a loss.

 Content link
Link to other sub-units

- Sub-units 5.5 and 3.3 are linked because the fixed and variable costs explained in 3.3 play a key role in the calculation of break-even.
- Sub-units 5.5 and 3.4 are linked because the trading account (the first part of the income statement) starts with the calculation of profit as sales revenue minus costs of sales.

Concept link

The concept of **change** is linked to the topic of break-even analysis because the break-even chart shows how changes in price or costs have an impact on break-even quantity and profit.

 Content link
Link to your IA

Even if your IA is not specifically about break-even, you can apply the contents of this unit to your chosen organization: do they use break-even methods? Why/why not?

5.6 PRODUCTION PLANNING HL ONLY

This sub-unit focuses on the process of planning production, organizing supply chains, implementing methods of stock control and calculating production ratios.

You should be able to:

✔ explain the local and global supply chain process

✔ contrast just-in-case (JIC) and just-in-time (JIT)

✔ construct and interpret stock control charts based on lead time, buffer stock, re-order level and re-order quantity

✔ calculate and interpret:

    ✔ capacity utilization rate   ✔ defect rate

    ✔ labour productivity   ✔ capital productivity

    ✔ productivity rate   ✔ operating leverage

    ✔ cost to buy (CTB)   ✔ cost to make (CTM).

HL

Topic summary

The **supply chain** is the system of connected organizations, information, logistics, resources, and activities that a business needs to reach its customers. It includes several external stakeholders: the suppliers, distributors and retailers. Supply chains can be short and local (which is more sustainable) or long and international, involving exports and imports (which is less sustainable).

The two **methods of stock control** are:

- **Just-in-case (JIC)**: a traditional method where stock levels of raw materials and of finished products are high, in case of a sudden increase in demand.

- **Just-in-time (JIT)**: a more modern method where raw materials are supplied only when necessary, and where goods are produced only when there is an order, without stock of finished products.

JIC and JIT both have advantages and disadvantages – for example JIC may reduce costs by buying in bulk and getting discounts from suppliers, but JIT does not require storage space.

Holding stock can be expensive; several elements must be taken into consideration when deciding on stock control, especially:

- Maximum stock level.

- Minimum stock level (also called "**buffer stock**").

- **Lead time** (between ordering new stock of raw materials and receiving it).

- Optimal stock level.

- Re-order level and re-order quantity.

- Nature of stock (may be perishable).

In order to know how efficient a facility is, production managers can calculate its **capacity utilization rate**:

$$\text{Capacity utilization rate} = \frac{\text{Actual output}}{\text{Maximum productive capacity}} \times 100$$

To measure the efficiency of production, managers can also calculate the **productivity rate**:

$$\text{Productivity rate} = \frac{\text{Total output}}{\text{Total input}} \times 100$$

In certain contexts, the following four calculations can be useful too:

Defect rate: the percentage of output (units) that fail to meet quality standards

$$\text{defect rate} = \frac{\text{number of defective units}}{\text{total output}} \times 100$$

Labour productivity, to measure the efficiency of a worker: the value or volume of output produced by a worker per unit of time (for example per hour or per day):

$$\text{Labour productivity} = \frac{\text{total output}}{\text{total hours worked}}$$

Capital productivity, to measure the efficiency of the company's capital, especially its working capital:

$$\text{working capital productivity} = \frac{\text{sales revenue}}{\text{current assets} - \text{current liabilities}}$$

Operating leverage, the ratio of fixed costs to variable costs to calculate how well a company uses its fixed costs to generate income:

$$\text{Operating leverage} = \frac{\text{quantity} \times (\text{price} - \text{variable cost per unit})}{\text{quantity} \times (\text{price} - \text{variable cost per unit}) - \text{fixed costs}}$$

One business decision is whether to buy or to make: it may sometimes be cheaper for a business to buy a product made elsewhere, and even to import it, rather than manufacture it.

- **CTB (cost to buy)** is calculated by multiplying Price by Quantity.

- **CTM (cost to make)** is calculated by multiplying Variable Costs by Quantity, and adding Fixed Costs.

$$\text{CTB} = \text{P} \times \text{Q}$$

$$\text{CTM} = (\text{CV} \times \text{Q}) + \text{FC}$$

>> Assessment tip

If you have to calculate a ratio (such as capacity utilization rate or productivity rate), do not forget to include the percentage sign in your answer. Even if the calculation is correct, without the % sign you would not achieve the maximum mark.

>> Revision tip

As you revise this sub-unit, you should identify some companies you know that use JIC and some others that use JIT, and explain why: does it depend on the sector, on the type and size of business, on its culture, on its marketing or finance? These examples will help you consolidate your knowledge of the differences between JIT and JIC.

Content link
Link to your IA

Even if your IA is not about operations management, you could apply the contents of this sub-unit to your chosen organization. How would you describe their supply chain? How do they control their stock? Can you calculate their capacity utilization rate or some other rates?

Content link
Link to other sub-units

- Sub-unit 4.5 about the P for Place of the marketing mix refers to different types of distribution channels, according to the number of intermediaries.

- Sub-unit 5.3 (HL only) about lean management refers to the topic of JIT as JIT is one of the methods enabling companies to be "lean" and more efficient.

Concept link

The concepts of **change**, **sustainability** and **creativity** are linked to the topic of production planning:

- **Change** because calculating production ratios (and comparing trends or industry benchmarks) may help managers understand what needs to be changed to improve productivity and efficiency (for example: training staff to improve labour productivity).

- **Sustainability** because JIT can help companies become less wasteful.

- **Creativity** because the supply chain may always be subject to innovation and improvement: JIT itself was innovative when it was first developed in Japan in the 1960s and 1970s.

5.7 CRISIS MANAGEMENT AND CONTINGENCY PLANNING   HL ONLY

You should be able to:

✔ distinguish between crisis management and contingency planning

✔ analyse factors that affect effective crisis management

✔ analyse the impact of contingency planning for a given organization or situation.

This sub-unit focuses on organizations' abilities to deal with severe problems.

HL

Topic summary

Crisis management is a direct response to a specific, unpredictable event, whereas **contingency planning** refers to an organization's efforts to minimize the effects of a potential crisis.

The main factors that affect crisis management are:

- Communication from senior managers.

- Transparency: telling stakeholders the truth.

- Speed: in both actions and communication.

- Control of the impacts.

Not every crisis can be anticipated, but contingency planning is about being prepared, in advance, just in case; four impacts are important for contingency planning:

- Risks: what risks, to whom, and how likely are they? (This is called "risk assessment" and organizations may prepare a "risk assessment register".)

- Cost: contingency planning may be costly, but less so than dealing with the crisis.

- Time: contingency planning takes time, especially for preparation.

- Safety: contingency planning must put safety first.

≫ Revision tip

As you revise this sub-unit, you should consider real crises that have recently affected business organizations, either locally, near you, or on a global scale. The different areas of the STEEPLE framework can give you a starting point: it could be a political crisis, an economic crisis, an ecological crisis etc.

🔗 Content link
Link to other sub-units

- Sub-unit 2.3 as leaders and managers are responsible for contingency planning and dealing with crises, should they occur.

- 2.6 as communication (both internally and externally) is essential in a crisis in order to keep all stakeholders informed.

- Sub-unit 3.9 (HL only) about budgets as companies usually set reserve funds aside to deal with any crisis.

🔗 Content link
Link to your IA

Even if your IA is not about operations management, you could apply the contents of this sub-unit to your chosen organization. Have they been affected by some external or internal crises in the past? Do they have contingency plans? Who is responsible for crisis management and contingency planning?

Concept link

The concepts of **ethics** and **change** are linked to the topic of crisis management:

- **Ethics**, because stakeholders expect transparency in communication (this was an issue in large-scale scandals such as the 2001 Enron accounting fraud and the 2010 BP Deepwater Horizon oil spill).

- **Change**, because some entrepreneurs may be less interested in contingency planning than in risk-taking, yet good business acumen is about thinking both optimistically and pessimistically about all possible changes, the best ones and the worst ones alike.

5.8   RESEARCH AND DEVELOPMENT   HL ONLY

This sub-unit focuses on the importance of R&D (research and development) in all organizations, no matter how big or small they are.

You should be able to:

✔ discuss the importance of research and development (R&D) for a business

✔ explain the importance of developing goods and services that address customers' unmet needs

✔ explain intellectual property protection, patents, copyrights and trademarks

✔ explain the difference between incremental innovation and disruptive innovation.

HL   Topic summary

Research and development (R&D) is important in all industries. Large businesses often have departments called "R&D", but innovation occurs in all sectors and in all organizations: even a small local bakery can be innovative, offering new cakes and new types of bread. R&D is not just about technology: all companies engage in R&D in their own way.

The aim is to develop goods and services that address customers' unmet needs. Successful R&D has many advantages for a business, such as enhancing the image of the company and motivating the workforce; there are disadvantages too, such as opportunity costs as investing in R&D means not investing in other areas such as promotion and professional development (staff upskilling).

Intellectual property rights (IP rights) are defined by the WTO (World Trade Organization) as "the rights given to persons over the creations of their minds". It is helpful to distinguish between:

- **Copyrights** giving protection to the author from the unlawful copying of the material they created.

- A **patent** is an exclusive right granted for an invention, so a form of protection excluding competitors from copying and commercial the exact same product.

- A **trademark** is another form of IP rights, typically for logos, slogans, designs, and phrases that help customers recognize a brand.

Innovation is an essential part of R&D. There are several types of innovation, for example 'product innovation' and 'process innovation', as well as:

- **'incremental innovation':** slight, gradual change to a product or a service, as opposed to 'radical innovation'

- **'disruptive innovation'** so strong and impactful that it changes the whole industry.

Numerous factors may influence R&D in an organization, such as organizational culture, technology, resources and past experience.

Content link
Link to other sub-units

- Sub-unit 4.4 as market research is essential for R&D, for example to collect customer feedback on existing products.

- Sub-unit 4.5 as extension strategies are often the result of R&D efforts.

Concept link

All four concepts are linked to the topic of research and development:

- **Creativity**, because innovation is at the core of R&D.

- **Ethics**, because research is sometimes based on practices that may be regarded as unethical, such as testing new pharmaceutical drugs and cosmetics on animals.

- **Sustainability,** as R&D departments increasingly explore ways to develop more sustainable products and processes.

- **Change**, because R&D is an ongoing process of creation, over time, of new products and new systems, ceaselessly changing the portfolio of the goods and services that the organization offers.

Content link
Link to your IA

Even if your IA is not about operations management, you could apply the contents of this sub-unit to your chosen organization: where do innovation, research and development take place in your organization? Is there a particular department or group of people responsible for it? Can you give examples of innovations they have implemented over time?

5.9 MANAGEMENT INFORMATION SYSTEMS HL ONLY

This sub-unit introduces the most recent technological and digital developments that are affecting the world of business, from the growth of e-commerce to 'digital Taylorism'.

You should be able to:

- ✔ define key terms related to information systems management: database, data mining and data analytics

- ✔ examine how companies use data mining and data analytics to inform decision-making, create customer loyalty programmes, and monitor their employees

- ✔ define cybercrime and cybersecurity

- ✔ analyse some of the critical infrastructures that are part of advanced computer technologies: artificial neural networks, data centres and cloud computing

- ✔ distinguish between big data, virtual reality, the internet of things and artificial intelligence

- ✔ evaluate the benefits, risks and ethical implications of advanced computer technologies and technological innovation on business decision-making and stakeholders.

HL | Topic summary

An information system (IS) is composed of **digital databases** that record information. Advanced information systems enable two related practices: data mining and data analytics. **Data mining** is the process of finding trends, patterns, and correlations within large datasets. **Data analytics** is the process of inspecting and modelling data in order to discover information; it shares many similarities with data mining, though the aim is not to find any hidden pattern nor to test some hypothesis, as in data mining, but just to reach conclusions based on the analysis of the raw data collected. Data mining and data analytics have many functions:

- In marketing, they can help managers make informed decisions, for example about market research, collecting data through customer loyalty programmes that record all purchases.

- In HRM, they can help monitor employees, by recording who does what and when. This use of digital technology to monitor workers is called **Digital Taylorism**.

Organizations increasingly make use of advanced computer technologies, such as **cloud computing** (the delivery of services via the internet, for example data storage, networking and software) hosted in **data centres** (buildings designed to house computer systems and their components). In the business world, these technologies have supported the growth of e-commerce in all its forms (Business to Business B2B, Business to Customer B2C, Customer to Customer C2C).

Some areas are in the growth phase of their lifecycle, for example the use of **'big data'** (extremely large databases that can be analysed to show trends and patterns) and the **internet of things** (IoT, the network of connected devices that transmit data to one another without human involvement). Others are still in their developmental phase, such as **virtual reality** (VR, the creation of simulated three-dimensional environments) for commercial purposes, **artificial neural networks** (ANN, an element of a computing system designed to simulate how the human brain analyses and processes information) and **artificial intelligence** (AI, the ability of computers and robots to mimic humans, especially how humans think and process information).

With the increasing use of all those innovations, many risks are present, such as **cybercrime** and breaches of **cybersecurity** (the practice of defending IT systems against malicious attacks) on the one hand, and ethical issues of privacy, confidentiality and anonymity on the other hand.

Content link

Link to your IA

Even if your IA is not about operations management, you can research how your chosen organization is making use of advanced information systems and digital technologies. Do they use e-commerce? Are cybercrime and data protection a concern for them? Do they employ methods of data mining and data analytics? The organization you chose for your IA gives you the chance to learn more about the contents of this sub-unit in context.

Test yourself

Can you explain the difference between database, data mining, data analytics, and 'big data'?

Content link

Link to other sub-units

- Sub-unit 2.4 presents Taylor and the 'original form' of Taylorism as the scientific management of human resources.

- Sub-unit 4.5 describes customer loyalty in marketing terms about promotion; customer loyalty schemes ensure repeat sales, but more importantly they help create databases about customers.

- Sub-unit 5.8 (HL only) explains the importance of R&D, which may use data mining and data analytics to better understand customers and therefore generate more sales, maximising revenue, profit and dividends.

Assessment tip

You do not need to memorize specific definitions for all the key terms in this sub-unit (such as 'artificial intelligence' or 'virtual reality'), but you must be able to explain them in your own words.

Concept link

The concepts of **creativity** and **ethics** are particularly relevant:

- **Creativity**, because engineers who work on AI and VR need to be creative to push the boundaries of science and technology.

- **Ethics**, because all technological and digital developments have ethical implications, for example regarding data protection, privacy and confidentiality.

INTERNAL ASSESSMENT

Your task

The IA in business management is the same for SL and HL students: same task and same criteria.

Your task

Your IA task is a **research project** about a real issue or problem facing a particular organization, using a conceptual lens:

- **conceptual lens** refers to the four key concepts: **change**, **creativity**, **ethics**, **sustainability**. You have to choose one of those concepts and write your research project focusing on that concept.

- **real issue or problem facing a particular organization** means that you must choose a real organization and write about an issue they currently encounter; it cannot be fictional or hypothetical. You may choose any type of organization (see sub-unit 1.2): it could be a multinational company, it could be a social enterprise, it could be a partnership or a cooperative etc.

You will formulate a **research question** and select three to five **Supporting Documents (SD)** that will help you answer your research question. In your IA, you will use extracts from those SD, citing them, analysing them, in order to reach your conclusions. SD are typically articles from business news, extracts of a company's official documents, such as their website or their annual report, or publications by organizations such as governments or NGOs. You could also decide to do primary research, for example to carry out interviews or use questionnaires to do surveys and collect data yourself.

The IA assesses your knowledge and understanding of the course, so you will use a range of tools (from the toolkit and/or the units of the course) and relevant business management terms and theories.

The aim of the task is that you engage with a contemporary business issue, and with recent authentic business documents. The format of the IA task is close to the "essay" format of writing that you are familiar with, with an introduction, a main body composed of different sections, and a conclusion.

What the IA is	What the IA is not
The opportunity to focus on **one concept** (for example, **sustainability** or **ethics**).	It does **not** focus on a hypothetical business idea or on a business proposal.
The chance to explore **one organization** that interests you (small or large, profit making or not!), one that you may know already, that you like, or one that intrigues you.	It is **not** a massive undertaking. You are expected to spend around 20 hours on your IA; this includes the time researching your topic, choosing your supporting documents, analysing your findings and writing up your IA.

What the IA is	What the IA is not
The opportunity to show your **subject knowledge**, i.e. your ability to use accurate terminology (words like stakeholders), models (such as the Ansoff matrix) and theories (such as motivation theories).	It is **not** an extended essay: you are not expected to go beyond the syllabus.
The chance to do **research** through genuine documents about business management – and not documents (or websites!) written for students.	It is **not** about finding out and copying ready-made analyses (e.g. a ready-made SWOT analysis of a well-known business).

Frequently Asked Questions

Should I do primary research?	Doing primary research is possible but not compulsory. It is a very good way to collect first-hand information, for example if you interview a business owner. However, primary research has several limits – for example, if you carry out a survey, how representative is your sample? To what extent can you generalise to the whole population?
Do I have to include finance and calculations in my IA?	There is no requirement to include finance and calculations – in the same way, there is no requirement to include marketing or human resources. This depends on your research question: the tools and theories you use must be relevant. If your research question is about ethical aspects of recruitment, financial aspects probably won't be relevant; however if your research question is about changes in pricing strategies, financial aspects will be relevant.
How many tools and theories should I use?	There is no requirement about the number of tools and theories. Again, it depends on your research question. Moreover, the size and length of all the tools vary a lot: if you calculate a profit margin, this is one line, but if you apply the Ansoff matrix to an organization, this can easily take more than one page!
Do I need appendices?	There is no requirement to include appendices. You may want to include extra material as an appendix, for example if you prepared a full STEEPLE as part of your background preparation, but material in an appendix is not taken into account to award marks. Many students do not include appendices; it is allowed but not necessary.
What happens if I write more than 1800 words?	Anything above the 1800 words limit is not taken into account. For example, if you write 1900 words, the last 100 words are not considered; if those 100 words are your conclusion, your conclusion will not be read (and you will score zero for your conclusion!).
What is the minimum word length of the IA?	There is no minimum word length, though if your IA is much below the word limit, you may not have sufficiently developed all your ideas … and maybe you should then ask yourself: what else could I add? You have an allowance of 1800 words – use it!
Do I need to state the concept in my research question?	The word itself ("**ethics**" or "**sustainability**") does not need to be in your research question, but you must indicate it on the cover page.
Where do I start? Should I write my research question and then search for relevant, supporting documents, or should I collect supporting documents before I write my question?	It is an organic process: you may need to do both at the same time! Once you have chosen your organization and your concept, you should do some initial research to see what has recently been published on that theme. Your findings will help you choose a topic, you may then have a first possible research question, but it is not necessarily the final one. You may realise that you need better documents but as you read more documents, your research question could slightly change too. What matters is that you have "a fit" between the research question and the documents that will help you answer it – this takes time!

Examples of possible IA titles

This table shows you how, for the same organization (Lego, in this case), you could formulate very different research questions, depending on your conceptual lens and the topic that interests you.

Chosen concept: **change**	How has Lego grown beyond physical blocks into a toy empire?
	How did Lego change its strategy, as it almost went bankrupt, to become one of the most powerful brands in the world?
	Should Lego change production to non-plastic blocks, such as wood?
	How effectively have recent changes in Lego's marketing strategy boosted its profitability?
Chosen concept: **creativity**	How is Lego's "Rebuild the World" Campaign impacting its brand image?
	How does Lego enhance the consumer experience?
	Is Lego's shift in marketing strategies enough to maintain its market position in a rising trend of digital play?
	What does the success of Lego teach us about creativity?
Chosen concept: **ethics**	Does Lego ethically market its toys?
	How has Lego responded to criticism that it targets boys as consumers and not children of all gender identities?
	To what extent has Lego removed gender bias?
	Should Lego integrate ethics into its communication strategy with customers?
Chosen concept: **sustainability**	Can Lego genuinely claim to be sustainable?
	How can "Lego Replay" help to boost its market share in the US?
	How can Lego meet its sustainability goals without hurting profitability?
	Should Lego continue to focus its research and development on recyclable bricks?

About the selection of your Supporting Documents (SDs)

Your SDs are very important for two reasons:

1. They give you the contents of your IA, the ideas that you will use and analyse (whether you quote them directly or not). They are at the core of your IA.

2. They are also directly assessed through criterion B: up to 4 marks (out of 25), as explained later in this section. For 4 marks, they need to be sufficiently in depth with a range of perspectives.

If I do primary research, what does it mean for my SDs?	If you have carried out one interview, you must include a transcript (i.e. the full text) as one of your SDs. If you have done a survey, a copy of your questionnaire must be included, and it counts as one SD.
May I use an audio file or a video as an SD?	An audio file or video may be used as an SD, you must then include the transcript (the full text) as one of your SDs. If the file is very long, you only need to include the transcript of the relevant part. Note that a maximum of one SD may be a transcript of video or audio material.
How long should my SD be?	SDs should not be very long documents – typically 2 pages (A4) each, a maximum of 5 pages. If you want to use a very long document, for example the annual report of a company, then you should only select the relevant section for your IA, i.e. the section that you will use and quote. In total, the file with your SDs should be 25 pages maximum. You should aim to present it well, clearly labelling each SD and indicating the exact source using a conventional referencing system (APA, MLA, Harvard etc).

The instructions state that I have to highlight some passages – what does it mean?	As each SD will be a few pages long, you may not use every single sentence in your IA; for example, an online news article where you will only use some facts mentioned in the first and last paragraph. You then literally highlight (for example in yellow) those sentences to show the reader what you have selected and used in that SD.
How recent should my SDs be?	Your SDs must be recent: they must be published within a maximum of three years prior to the submission of your IA to the IB. For example, if your IA is submitted in April 2024, the documents must be published between April 2021 and April 2024. Of course, they may refer to facts and data prior to that period.
May I use a document written in another language?	SDs may be originally written in any language, but you must translate the passages that you highlight and then quote or use in your work.

The assessment criteria

Your teacher will mark your IA using seven criteria, A to G:

- Criterion A assesses the way you integrate the **concept** in your IA.

- Criterion B assesses your selection of **Supporting Documents (SD)**.

- Criterion C assesses your selection and application of **tools and theories**.

- Criterion D assesses your **analysis and evaluation**.

- Criterion E assesses your **conclusions**.

- Criterion F assesses the **structure** of your IA.

- Criterion G assesses the **presentation** of your IA.

Criterion A: Integration of concept (up to 4 marks)

To achieve a high mark for A, your concept must be well integrated throughout your IA, from your introduction to your conclusion. A concept is an abstract idea, but with your IA, you can explore the meaning and importance of this concept more concretely, in the context of an organization, and not just in theory.

▲ Mention your concept often in your IA, as this will help you keep it in mind; otherwise you could focus too much on other aspects, such as your tools, to the detriment of the concept itself.

Criterion B: Supporting Documents (up to 4 marks)

To achieve a high mark for B, your SD must (i) be relevant, (ii) be sufficiently in-depth and (iii) provide a range of ideas and views. This latter aspect is essential for 4 marks: your sources must give different perspectives, for example internal (from the organization) *vs* external (from news article), or quantitative *vs* qualitative, or local *vs* global, or for *vs* against etc.

▲ Make sure that you have 3, 4 or 5 SDs: not fewer, and not more. Every year, some candidates lose marks because they do not have the right number of supporting documents.

Criterion C: Selection and application of tools and theories (up to 4 marks)

To achieve a high mark for C, you must use appropriate tools and theories from the course contents and from the toolkit (see pages 137–144). You should also use subject terminology throughout, i.e. words such as "stakeholders", "franchising", "outsourcing", "B2B" etc.

▲ Do not try to go around the word length by creating tables (for example around a SWOT analysis) claiming that the words inside the table do not count because there is a frame around them.

Criterion D: Analysis and evaluation (up to 5 marks)

To achieve a high mark for D, you must select relevant data from your SD (for example facts, figures, quotes), analyse them (using your chosen tools, see criterion C above) and integrate your findings coherently. Consider also possible bias and assumptions, depending on the sources and their perspectives.

▲ Do not analyse each SD separately, but combine them in your IA.

▲ Start your conclusion by copying the research question: this will help you ensure that you answer it precisely in your conclusion! Every year, some candidates achieve 2 marks rather than 3 marks because they do not answer their research question. Their conclusion is on the same topic, but they have deviated from their original question.

▲ Be careful of websites that suggest IA structures. Like for the EE, there is no prescribed structure for the IA: it will depend on the research question, on the concept and on the organization.

▲ Make the layout look professional and 'business-like': ensure that you submit a document to the IB which has a high standard of presentation and reflects well on you, as a student of business management!

Criterion E: Conclusions (up to 3 marks)

To achieve a high mark for E, your conclusion must explicitly answer your research question. It must be consistent with the evidence that you have presented, with your analysis and with your findings. If you have contrasting arguments, this is where you can weigh them up, for example advantages vs disadvantages. This is why closed questions ("should company x do y?") are often better for an IA, because the answer will be clear: "Yes …" or "No …"; open questions (such as "to what extent …") are harder to answer in 1800 words; they may be better for an extended essay. Your conclusion should not be too short and too superficial; its length should be a good paragraph or two, up to half a page.

Criterion F: Structure (up to 2 marks)

To achieve a high mark for F, the structure of your IA should be appropriate, coherent, logical and easy to follow, for example "Part 1: reasons in favour of the merger of companies A and B", followed by "Part 2: reasons against the merger of the two companies".

Criterion G: Presentation (up to 2 marks)

To achieve a high mark for G, your work should be well presented. Several formal and structural elements must be included: a title page, an accurate table of contents, appropriate headings and sub-headings and numbered pages. You should also make sure you reference all your sources, which could be with footnotes or in-text citation with a bibliography at the end.

EXTERNAL ASSESSMENT

This section is composed of four parts:

✔ **Paper 1**: key aspects, tips and strategies to answer the 10 marks question.

✔ **Paper 2**: key aspects, tips and a full practice paper.

✔ **Paper 3**: key aspects, tips and a full practice paper.

✔ **Command terms**: what they mean and what examiners expect.

PAPER 1 OVERVIEW

Paper 1 is the same for SL and HL. This means that all questions are about SL (core) parts of the course, so there won't be questions about HL-only topics such as organizational culture, budgets or crisis management.

Three months before the examination, the IB will release a short extract (around 200 words) of a case study of a fictional organization. The extract will help you discover the context of the organization, for example where it is located or in which economic sector it operates. The extract will be accompanied by a list of keywords and business topics on which you should do some preparatory research, for example to have some general ideas about the industry, or the keywords. There won't be questions about the keywords, but you will need them to understand the case study.

At the start of the examination, you will receive the full case study (a couple of pages long, including the passages that you already know) and the questions themselves. Most questions will be qualitative, although there might be some questions involving some calculations.

The first section of paper 1 (called **Section A**) is worth 20 marks; it is composed of a series of short questions, such as:

- Define the term stakeholders (line xx). [2 marks]

- Outline one external growth method that ABC could use. [2 marks]

- Explain two strategies that ABC could use to solve its cash-flow problems. [4 marks]

- Distinguish between two types of rewards, other than salary, that ABC could offer its night shift workers. [6 marks]

You will not be asked to define business terms that are not in the course (terms such as "mortgage", "consultant" or "blockchain"), but you must be ready to define all the business terms that are used in the course and in this book!

Line numbers are included in brackets when the question refers to a specific passage (for example, a term to define, so you can see it in context).

The command terms (such as define, outline, explain) have specific meanings, as explained at the end of this section.

All the questions of Section A are compulsory and cover a range of topics, so you should not avoid revising some sections of the course, in the hope that they won't come up in the exam!

The second section of paper 1 (called **Section B**) is worth 10 marks; you have to answer one question worth 10 marks. You have a choice of two.

QUESTIONS WORTH 10 MARKS

The task

Besides shorter questions worth 2 marks, 4 marks or 6 marks (the ones that start with command terms such as "define", "calculate" or "explain"), for paper 1 (SL and HL) and for paper 2 (SL and HL), you have to answer one question worth 10 marks. This requires different skills and a different approach, as explained in this section.

▼ **Table 6.1.1** Examples of questions worth 10 marks

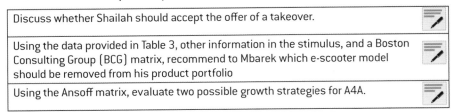

Discuss whether Shailah should accept the offer of a takeover.
Using the data provided in Table 3, other information in the stimulus, and a Boston Consulting Group (BCG) matrix, recommend to Mbarek which e-scooter model should be removed from his product portfolio
Using the Ansoff matrix, evaluate two possible growth strategies for A4A.

These questions have two main features:

1. They always start with evaluative command terms such as "discuss", "recommend" or "evaluate", the task is more demanding and your answer will be longer, more structured, more developed.

2. They always refer to stimulus material and thus to an organization or some of its stakehholders, which is why there are references to "Shailah", "Mbarek" and "A4A" in the questions above.

Your answer will be *at least* one page long, and probably much more in order to achieve a high mark. If your answer is too short, you will not sufficiently develop the different points and arguments.

Because of the time/marks ratio, you should **spend at least 20 minutes** on such questions.

Assessment markbands

The examiners use markbands for these questions, so it is important that you understand the criteria in advance: this way, you know what the examiner expects in your answer.

For these questions, the IB markbands are as follows:

▼ **Table 6.1.2** The assessment markbands for questions worth 10 marks

Marks	Level descriptor
0	The work does not reach a standard described by the descriptor.
1–2	• Little understanding of the demands of the question. • Little use of business management tools and theories; any tools and theories that are used are irrelevant or used inaccurately. • Little or no reference to the stimulus material. • No arguments are made.
3–4	• Some understanding of the demands of the question. • Some use of business management tools and theories, but these are mostly lacking in accuracy and relevance. • Superficial use of information from the stimulus material, often not going beyond the name of the person(s) or name of the organization. • Any arguments made are mostly unsubstantiated.
5–6	• The response indicates an understanding of the demands of the question, but these demands are only partially addressed. • Some relevant and accurate use of business management tools and theories. • Some relevant use of information from the stimulus material that goes beyond the name of the person(s) or name of the organization but does not effectively support the argument. • Arguments are substantiated but are mostly one-sided.
7–8	• Mostly addresses the demands of the question. • Mostly relevant and accurate use of business management tools and theories. • Information from the stimulus material is generally used to support the argument, although there is some lack of clarity or relevance in some places. • Arguments are substantiated and have some balance.
9–10	• Clear focus on addressing the demands of the question. • Relevant and accurate use of business management tools and theories. • Relevant information from the stimulus material is integrated effectively to support the argument. • Arguments are substantiated and balanced, with an explanation of the limitations of the case study or stimulus material.

Source: IB *Business management guide*

QUESTION PRACTICE

Example 1

To highlight the difference between a "good answer" (markband for 7–8 marks) and a "very good answer" (markband for 9–10 marks), we will consider the following question.

The question is about a chain of hotels called *Dales*. In 2020, in order to remain competitive, *Dales* outsourced the cleaning of hotel rooms to a company called *Wire*. Recent customer feedback, however, has highlighted concerns about room cleanliness at *Dales* hotels – so *Dales* is now considering whether it should stop outsourcing the cleaning service.

Recommend if *Dales* should stop outsourcing the cleaning of hotel rooms. [10]

Assessment tip

To score 9–10 rather than 7–8, you should do the following:

1 Refer to the impacts of business decisions. The question here is "Recommend if *Dales* should stop outsourcing the cleaning of hotel rooms"; what would be the implications of stopping outsourcing and of not stopping outsourcing? If *Dales* stops outsourcing its cleaners, the costs are likely to rise but they would be able to monitor and improve quality – very good answers will refer to this.

2 Explain and justify the tool and theories you use in the answer: for example, if you refer to staff turnover rate, tell the examiner why you believe it is relevant (a high turnover rate means high costs for ongoing recruitment and training).

3 Use business terminology: show the examiner that you can use terms such as "profit", "wages", "recruitment", "competitive environment" and "quality".

4 Quote short extracts of the case study to help make a point: here, a very good answer would refer to the fact that "*Dales* is positioned as a high-price and high-quality hotel chain", so guests have very high expectations regarding the cleanliness of the rooms – and outsourcing could then help with quality management.

5 Ensure your entire answer is balanced: balanced not only regarding the arguments for and against stopping outsourcing, but also possibly balancing quantitative and qualitative elements, and in this case finance versus human resources.

6 Justify your judgments and your final recommendation: provide evidence and justification for all the points that you make, using elements from the case study (quoting it) as well as your knowledge of business management – in this case: the advantages and disadvantages of outsourcing.

SAMPLE STUDENT ANSWER

The following answer is therefore a **very good answer**, reaching the markband for 9–10 marks.

Note: in the commentary provided here, the numbers 1 to 6 refer to the numbers given in the assessment tip above.

Dales hotels have several problems of brand image and reputation: customers are not happy with customer service, food quality and room cleanliness – and all this explains why room booking and profit have decreased so much. To address the issue of room cleanliness, *Dales* could decide to stop subcontracting to *Wire* – and to "insource" this service again.

Option 1: *Dales* stops outsourcing

On the one hand, if *Dales* stops outsourcing its cleaners, costs will rise, as outsourcing did cut costs (from 5% of room revenues to 2%) – so insourcing would be more expensive, both for the variable costs (per room) and fixed costs too (the costs of recruiting and training cleaners). These costs may be even higher, as the high staff turnover rate amongst cleaners means that recruitment and training would be ongoing. In the short term, this means that *Dales*' overall profit (which is already low) would be hit (and may even turn into loss). On the other hand,

▲ This is a reference to implications (1).

▲ The tools used are explained (2).

the quality of room cleanliness may improve, and Dales would be able to control this, training its own cleaners to the right standards, without relying on Wire's own systems and practices, which are below Dales' benchmarks. This is a problem as Dales is "positioned as a high-price and high-quality chain" so in the luxury market where guests are very demanding.

▲ Use of subject terminology all along (3).

▲ Short extracts of the case study are quoted to help make a point (4).

Option 2: Dales continues outsourcing
Financially, outsourcing has enabled Dales to save some money, which is very important at this moment in time, when bookings are going down. If finance is the priority, outsourcing is the best strategy, but Dales' managers should speak to Wire about the declining quality and guests' complaints. The cleaners employed by Wire must work to satisfy Dales' hotel guests, as Dales is their customer – or Dales could contact other cleaning companies and see how much it would cost, and whether they would provide better service. There may be other local companies offering the same services as Wire.

▲ Balanced arguments all along (5).

In conclusion, we can see that both options have advantages and disadvantages. Insourcing may seem a good idea, but it will only solve one of Dales' problems; there are other factors that contribute to the falling room occupancy rate: the quality of food and the quality of customer service. Dales should adopt a total quality management approach in order to make improvements in all areas, and not just consider the cleanliness as an isolated factor.

▲ The judgments are substantiated, using both data from the case study and knowledge from the business syllabus (6).

This response could have achieved 9/10 marks.

Example 2

To apply the generic markband to a specific question, we will consider the following question.

The case study here is about Sam's small business (called AFA) that successfully sells fair trade products in some stores and via e-commerce. Sam has just been offered a takeover by a very large international retailer.

Discuss whether Sam should accept the offer of the takeover.   [10]

>> Assessment tip

In order to score 9 or 10 marks, you need to do the following:

IB criteria from the 9–10 markband	What this means for the question: "Discuss whether Sam should accept the offer of the takeover."
Clear focus on addressing the demands of the question.	You must show that you understand the task well…and that you do what the question is requiring you to do. The command term "discuss" means "offer a considered and balanced review that includes a range of arguments, factors or hypotheses. Opinions or conclusions should be presented clearly and supported by appropriate evidence". Here you are asked to weigh up the reasons why Sam should accept the takeover versus the reasons why he should not accept it.
Relevant and accurate use of business management tools and theories.	You must show that you know the meaning of takeover (as a form of acquisition) as well as the advantages and disadvantages of this method of external growth, and the associated risks. In your answer, you are likely to use other parts of the syllabus, beyond "1.5 Growth and evolution" about takeover — for example you could write about organizational structure, workers' motivation and stakeholder conflict (as a takeover may lead to problems of human resources management). When you plan your answer and write draft notes, consider the *entire* course, not just the topic of the question (here: takeover).
Relevant information from the stimulus material is integrated effectively to support the argument.	The word "effectively" means that you should not just copy passages from the stimulus material in your answer, but integrate them well in your answer. This is *not* an exercise of reading comprehension: the examiner is not going to assess if you can spot, in the text, the passages where relevant arguments are made. You may, of course, quote the stimulus, but this alone is not enough: remember, the examiner has the same text, and they will not give you extra marks just because you can quote it.
Arguments are substantiated and balanced, with an explanation of the limitations of the case study or stimulus material.	Write a *balanced* answer: for all these questions, there are always arguments for and against (here: reasons for the takeover, reasons against the takeover). For high marks, the examiner expects you to consider both sides. This does not mean that you will have the same number of arguments — for example, you could conclude that there are more arguments *against* the takeover than arguments *for* the takeover, and therefore that Sam should *not* accept the takeover…or the other way around! Such "discuss" questions do not have a right or wrong answer; what the examiner will reward is your ability to consider different perspectives, evaluate arguments and come up with a clear, specific, explicit conclusion. All the points you make in your answer should be directly linked to the question (here: the takeover) and justified (i.e. providing reasons, not just statements). For example, as part of your exam preparation, you may have prepared mock answers about leadership styles and you want to show the examiner that you know about them…but should you write about this? Yes, if you can link it to the topic of takeover, but if you cannot, it is better not to mention it. Your judgments must be relevant — and also substantiated: this means that they must be justified, validated, corroborated, with reference to the case study and to your knowledge of business management, in an objective way.

SAMPLE STUDENT ANSWER

The following very good answer meets all the criteria explained above:

▲ The candidate does not simply repeat what is in the stimulus material (for example about the strong online presence of the international retailer) but also makes deductions about what it means (for example in terms of source of finance and management systems).

> Selling AFA to a very large international retailer with a strong online presence can increase AFA's brand image and help it become more popular. A larger international retailer means that they have a better source of finance so that it can help AFA bigger in the market. It also means that the retailer has a better managing system to help AFA to deal

with the managerial problems. In addition, it might be able to help AFA to deal with the problem of decreasing gross profit margin. Also, the diseconomies of scale may be able to sort out by the large international retailer as they have a wider way to reach suppliers and they have a better ability to do bulk buying. As a whole, it will help AFA to grow and expand to a better stage and increase the brand reputation. However, all the advantages above are just an assumption. There is not so much information about the international retailer except a strong online presence. Is it selling for trade products? Does the managing system actually fit AFA's situation? Is the brand image of AFA able to remain by the new retailer? These are problems that Sam needs to think about carefully.

From Sam's perspective, right now there are huge disagreements between Sam and Finn which is not good for AFA operation. Sam's leadership style is totally different from Finn's and from the case study, it seems that Sam is not able to work well with Finn. This will also demotivate other employees are well. Therefore takeover can be one of the strategies to sort out the communication problems as Sam is no longer the leader of AFA. On the other hand, takeover can provide Sam a great deal of finance so that he can invest in other areas that he is interested in. Before there was a financial problem when Sam first started up his business, but now it won't be.

In this case, Sam is able to have enough fresh capital to start new innovative businesses. Other than this, the business growth was outstripping Sam and Finn's ability to manage which means Sam not actually fully capable of managing AFA. Taking over AFA by others can help Sam out.

However, this is the first business for Sam and he has put a lot of efforts for AFA's growth. Right now even the gross profit margin is declining but it is still acceptable. On the other hand, even though Sam sometimes has disagreements with Finn, the business still runs pretty well, at least it is growing. The future of AFA is unknown and if it is not good, it will be bad news for Sam if he accepts the offer of takeover.

▲ The candidate uses relevant subject terminology throughout, for example about "decreasing gross profit margin" and "diseconomies of scale".

▲ The candidate considers the issue from different perspectives, as different stakeholders may have different views. This approach often works very well.

▲ The candidate provides a balanced view, for example about both the disadvantages and the advantages for Sam.

▲ The candidate analyses the consequences of the different courses of action: writing "which means" is a good device to make links between ideas and to show the examiner that the candidate understands the different implications of business decisions.

▲ The candidate uses suitable terms such as "however" and "on the other hand" which enable them to contrast ideas, to fully discuss them, as opposed to writing a one-sided answer.

▲ The candidate pursues the logic of the structure they decided to give in the answer, i.e. considering different perspectives one after the other (from the manager's perspective, from the employees' perspective, from the customers' perspective…) This is also fully in line with the IB learner profile.

▲ The conclusion is clear and explicit: more advantages than disadvantages, so Sam should accept the offer (the opposite conclusion, not accepting the offer, would have been acceptable too, depending on the factors and elements emphasized by the candidate).

> From the employees' perspective, taking over is not good now for them as they might be fired, especially for Finn and Kim who also put a lot of efforts in AFA.
>
> However from the customer's perspective, this may be beneficial as the price of the fair trade products might be likely to decrease as AFA will be able to reach economies of scale and hence reduce the price.
>
> Overall, Sam should accept the offer as the advantages outweigh the disadvantages. Right now AFA is facing many problems, financial, managerial as well as the serving quality of the retail shops. The leaders of AFA seem not able to deal with all the problems and it should be better for AFA to pass on to the large international retailer for a better future and market share.

This response could have achieved 10/10 marks.

Note: The answer fulfils all the criteria for a maximum mark of 10/10. This does not mean that the answer is perfect – for example the candidate could have written a better introduction. Given the time constraints of the exam conditions, the examiner is not waiting for the perfect, ultimate, fully comprehensive answer in order to award 10/10.

PAPER 2 OVERVIEW

Paper 2 is different for SL and HL. Some questions may be common, but HL will have questions specifically about HL components of the course.

Paper 2 has a quantitative focus, which means that many questions will involve calculations (for example about investment appraisal or break-even analysis). There will also be some qualitative questions.

At the start of the examination, you will receive a booklet with some stimulus material (short texts, charts, tables, infographics, etc) and questions. You will write your answers directly in the booklet itself.

Practice Exam Paper 2

At this point, you will have re-familiarized yourself with the content of the IB business management syllabus. Additionally, you will have picked up some key techniques and skills to refine your exam approach. It is now time to put these skills to the test; in this section you will find a practice examination paper 2, with exactly the same structure as the exam you will complete at the end of the DP course. The only difference is the fact that, for your paper 2 exam, you will have to write your answers in the booklet provided.

Section A

Answer **all** questions from this section.

1. La Vaquita (LV)

In the Mexican state of Querétaro, a group of five dairy farmers have decided to set up a cooperative named *La Vaquita* (*LV*). Working together will enable them to achieve economies of scale. The cooperative's initial capital is $5000.

The farmers have forecasted the following figures for the first year of operation, beginning in July:

Sales

- Average selling price of each piece of cheese: $4.

- 3000 pieces of cheese will be sold in July, and 4000 pieces per month from August onwards.

- One half of the production will be sold directly to customers, who will pay cash, in the cooperative store. The other half will be sold to supermarkets, on credit, paid one month later.

Costs

- Rent: $4500 per month.

- Labour costs: $2500 per month.

- Raw materials: 30% of sales revenue every month.

- Overheads: $1100 every other month (starting in July).

    a)   Define the term cooperative.   [2]

    b)   Prepare a monthly cash flow forecast for *LV* for the first four months of operation (July to October).   [6]

    c)   Comment on *LV* cash flow forecast.   [2]

2. Company A's market share

Company A operates in a market where it has a market share of 12%.

15 other companies compete in the same market:

Company	Market share in %
Company B	3
Company C	17
Company D	6
Company E	3
Company F	5
Company G	5
Company H	9
Company I	4
Company J	6
Company K	3
Company L	8
Company M	5
Company N	3
Company O	1
Company P	10

    a)   Identify the mode and the median.   [2]

    b)   Calculate the average market share. Show your workings.   [2]

c) Comment on Company A's position in terms of quartile. [2]

d) If the entire market is worth $50m, calculate the sales revenue of Company A. Show your workings. [2]

e) Company A and C are going to merge. Construct a pie chart to represent the market share of that new company. [2]

Section B

Answer **one** question from this section.

3. Abhinav Awasthi's construction business

Abhinav Awasthi has a small construction business in Pune, India. With the help of his accountant, he has started to prepare the following figures for his final accounts.

Selected financial information, as at 31 May (all figures in $)

Cash	55 000
Cost of sales	3 000 000
Creditors	45 000
Expenses	2 300 000
Fixed assets	350 000
Retained profit	215 000
Sales revenue	5 600 000
Share capital	200 000
Short-term loan	10 000
Stock	50 000

He did not repay any loan interest nor any dividends.

a) Define the term *fixed assets*. [2]

b) Construct the profit and loss account of Abhinav's business. [4]

c) i) Calculate the current ratio. [2]

ii) Comment on the current ratio. [2]

Abhinav has worked as a sole trader for 7 years, since he opened his business. However, he is now thinking about changing this, and either registering as a private limited company, or creating a partnership with two cousins who also work in the construction industry.

d) Discuss which type of legal organization could be more appropriate for Abhinav. [10]

4. Barberia Checho

Barberia Checho is a barbershop located in Medellín, Colombia. Sergio Valdez, the owner, works as a sole trader.

a) Outline the economic sector in which Sergio works. [2]

Although there are many barbershops in the neighbourhood, *Barberia Checho* is very popular and very busy. Its normal opening hours are 11 am to 9 pm, but it often stays open later, until 10 pm or 11 pm, if there are more customers waiting to have their hair cut. Sergio is now considering expanding his business.

The first option is to buy and convert the shop next door. The purchase and the refurbishment would cost $300,000. Sergio estimates that he can earn an extra $70,000 per year.

b) Calculate the payback period of option 1. Show your workings. [2]

The second option is to lease an empty barbershop in a different neighbourhood. It is a 5-year contract costing $85.000 in total, and he can expect total returns of $50.000 per year.

c) Calculate the ARR of option 2. Show your workings. [2]

With option 2, the fixed costs would be $17.000 per year and the contribution per unit $15.

d) Calculate

i) the number of haircuts needed to break even, per year. [2]

ii) the number of haircuts needed to reach the target profit of $50.000 per year. [2]

Besides Sergio himself, there are two other barbers at *Barberia Checho*: Cesar and Fredy. However, they are not Sergio's employees in a traditional sense: he does not pay them, but rather they rent a space in his barbershop with a chair, mirror and dressing table. Each barber receives 50% of the price paid by the customers whose hair he cuts; the other 50% goes to Sergio. They have some flexibility, as they may choose which days they work.

Cesar and Fredy know that the success of *Barberia Checho* is largely due to their own reputation as excellent barbers, and they are now asking for more financial and non-financial rewards. Sergio hesitates. If he refuses, he fears that Cesar and Fredy may decide to leave and go to work for one of his competitors, but he has many direct costs and indirect costs, and the current model suits him.

e) Examine how Sergio could change his system of financial and non-financial rewards. [10]

PAPER 3 OVERVIEW   HL ONLY

Paper 3 is based on the case study of a social enterprise – completely unseen, unlike paper 1 (i.e. there is no pre-release material for paper 3). At the start of the examination, you will receive a case study composed of several documents about a social enterprise; these documents (called "resources") may include images, text, infographics, emails, online posts, newspaper articles, etc. You will have to spend time reading them to understand the case study – and you then have to answer three questions:

- Firstly, you will need to describe the human need met by the social enterprise. In your answer, you should mention Maslow's pyramid of needs in order to have a theoretical frame (for example: physiological needs such as food and shelter, safety needs such as health and security etc).

- Secondly, you will need to explain two of the challenges that the social enterprise is facing (for example: financial challenges if they require more funding, or branding about their image and reputation).

- Thirdly, you will need to recommend a possible plan of action for the social enterprise: What should they do in the short term, as a priority? Then what should they do over the next years, more strategically? In your answer, you will need to use all the documents provided as well as your knowledge of the course (for example you could decide to apply a model such as the Ansoff matrix or Porter's Generic Strategies).

This long answer will be assessed on the following four aspects:

- Your ability to use all the resources provided (criterion A, 4 marks),
- Your ability to apply business management tools and theories (criterion B, 4 marks),
- Your evaluative skills (criterion C, 6 marks),
- Your ability to sequence your ideas and action plan in a clear and coherent manner (criterion D, 3 marks).

It is now time to put your skills to the test; in this section you will find a practice examination paper 3, with the same structure as the external assessment you will complete at the end of the course.

Practice Exam Paper 3

Bienvenus

Bienvenus is a small social enterprise in the outskirts of Marseilles, France's second largest city after Paris. It supports migrants who recently arrived in the country and do not speak French.

Resource 1: Extract from the leaflet "Bienvenus: who are we?"

You are all welcome here, you are all *bienvenus!*

We are a safe space for all migrants, no matter where they are from, no matter their background, their origin or their religion.

We provide a range of services, including:

- French classes (all levels, including total beginners).
- Visits from lawyers who can help you with legal papers.
- Meetings with counsellors who can help you with coping with trauma.

All this is free for you:

We want to make you feel welcome, to make you feel *bienvenus*! Everybody who works here is a volunteer, except our amazing founder Nolven – whose office door is always open. Come say hello!

And if you just want to come to have a coffee or a hot meal, to meet other people and play cards, to use our wifi and our computers, you are *bienvenus* too!

Resource 2: Email from the CEO, Ms Nolven Fouque:

From: Nolven Fouque <nolven@bienvenus.org.fr>
To: All Recipients <volunteers_list@ bienvenus.org.fr>
Subject: News to share

Friends,

I have some good news and some bad news.

The good news is that last month, we helped 74 people who came here for the very first time – this is a record! It is heart-warming to know that we can help so many people!

The bad news is that the City Council has rejected our application for an increase in funding, so we still need to find other sources of income, or change our operations. All our expenses keep increasing, so if you have ideas, please come to see me, my office door is always open!

My very best,

Nolven

Resource 3: *Bienvenus* — last year's budget (all data in $)

	Budgeted figures	Actual figures	Variance
Income			
Funding from City Council	100 000	100 000	0
Donations	10 000	5 000	5 000 (A)
Fundraising events	8 000	5 000	3 000 (A)
Total income	118 000	110 000	8 000 (A)
Expenses			
Nolven's salary	20 000	20 000	0
Materials (incl. food)	20 000	30 000	10 000 (A)
Rent	40 000	45 000	5 000 (A)
Bills (energy, wifi etc)	10 000	20 000	10 000 (A)
Total expenses	90 000	115 000	25 000 (A)
Net income	28 000	(5 000)	33 000 (A)

Resource 4: Recent Twitter messages that refer to *Bienvenus*

> Martin Brieux ✔
> @MBrieux36 ···
>
> The city should stop funding organisations like Bienvenus: $100 000 just given to migrants! Shameful! Our local schools should receive this money instead! I want my tax money to go to whoever I choose!
>
> 💬 98   🔁 258   ♡ 2 143   👁 144.6K   ⬆

> Françoise Lemoine ✔
> @Françoise_Lemoine ···
>
> As a lawyer, I am so happy to give one afternoon of my time to volunteer at Bienvenus! Trust me, these people need me more than some of my other clients in Marseilles!
>
> 💬 342   🔁 679   ♡ 6 281   👁 566.9K   ⬆

> Dominique Ng ✔
> @TheBestDominique ···
>
> My own family were migrants – and my dad told me there was no support like Bienvenus at the time. What they do is amazing, but surely the public sector should provide these services?
>
> 💬 211   🔁 391   ♡ 431   👁 8.5K   ⬆

QUESTION PRACTICE

1. Using an appropriate business management theory, describe a human need met by the social enterprise *Bienvenus*. [2]

2. Explain **two** possible challenges facing *Bienvenus*. [6]

3. Using all the resources provided and your knowledge of business management, recommend a possible plan of action to ensure the sustainability of *Bienvenus* for the next five years. [17]

COMMAND TERMS

In the exam questions, **command terms** are the words that tell you how to approach the question, especially in terms of depth. It is crucial that you understand these terms correctly. Before you answer a question, you should:

- Underline the command term.
- Look at the mark weighting of that question.
- Match your answer to the depth required for the command term.

In business management, examiners often say that many candidates do not achieve high marks because they do not pay sufficient attention to the command terms.

Command terms fall into four categories:

1. Some command terms assess your ability to demonstrate **knowledge and understanding** of the subject. These are the most accessible questions, worth 2 or 4 marks.

Command term	IB definition	Sample question	Note the following:
Define	Give the precise meaning of a word, phrase, concept or physical quantity.	Define the term *current asset*. [2 marks]	For such definition questions, you are not expected to refer to the case study or stimulus material. Note: *all* the terms in the five units of the syllabus may be the subject of such a definition question, from "public sector" (1.2) to "data mining" (5.9).
Describe	Give a detailed account.	Describe two changes in the external environment that have affected *RDM*. [4 ~~marks~~]	These two command terms are frequently used in business management exam questions. The questions may seem easy, yet many candidates do not achieve full marks because they sometimes write answers that are too *theoretical* or too *superficial*.
Outline	Give a brief account or summary.	With reference to *RDM*, outline one advantage and one disadvantage of Jan's leadership style. [4 marks]	In this context, *theoretical* means that the candidate does not take the case study into account, but writes a generic answer. *Superficial* means that the answer is too short; the text written by the candidate may not have nor add value: only copying an extract from the case study is not enough. Put another way, candidates often miss marks because they approach these questions as "reading comprehension" and only lift relevant passages from the text. These command terms are about knowledge and understanding of business management, not knowledge and understanding of the case study.
State	Give a specific name, value or other brief answer without explanation or calculation.	State two reasons Neno could use to select a specific location for his new shop. [2 marks]	Your answer may be very brief, just a few words or bullet points.

2. Some command terms assess your ability to demonstrate **application and analysis**. This is a more demanding task; these questions are usually worth more marks and your answers must be longer.

Command term	IB definition	Sample question	Note the following:
Analyse	Break down in order to bring out the essential elements or structure.	Analyse Omar's decision to outsource the IT support.	Analysis requires a rigorous and systematic approach, as you have to pay attention to all aspects and their relationships with one another. The images of a chain (composed of several rings) or a tree (with roots, branches and leaves) can help you understand the idea of links and relationships.
Apply	Use an idea, equation, principle, theory or law in relation to a given problem or issue.	Apply the BCG matrix to Adriana's product portfolio.	Applying means making explicit links between "theory" and "practice": you show that you know the theory (for example, the BCG matrix here) and that you understand what it means for a specific business situation.
Comment	Give a judgment based on a given statement or result of a calculation.	Comment on the changes in the liquidiy ratios of Tendy's over the last 5 years.	When you are asked to comment on something, you need first to pay close attention to the data: there is usually a trend, a change or an anomaly that you are asked to spot and write about. IB business management examiners use the system called "OFR" which stands for "Own Figure Rule"; this means that you will achieve marks if you properly interpret your results, even if the results themselves are not correct.
Distinguish	Make clear the differences between two or more concepts or items.	Distinguish between the leadership styles of Sam and Finn. [6 marks]	This command term is frequently used in business management exam questions. One common reason why many candidates do not achieve high marks is that they write about A, then about B, instead of writing about the differences between A and B.
Explain	Give a detailed account including reasons or causes.	Explain two types of financial rewards, other than salary, that *RDM* might offer its engineers and computer scientists. [4 marks]	This command term is frequently used in business management exam questions. One common reason why many candidates do not achieve high marks is that they only describe facts, they do not write about the reasons behind these facts. In the example here, they would only describe the types of financial rewards (such as fringe payments and perks) without explaining why these financial rewards are appropriate for the company's engineers.

3. Some command terms assess your ability to demonstrate **synthesis and evaluation**. These questions are worth 10 marks. Your answers must be longer, as explained earlier in this section.

Command term	Definition	Sample question	Note the following:
Compare	Give an account of the similarities between two (or more) items or situations, referring to both (all) of them throughout.	Compare the leadership style of manager A and of manager B.	Should you have an exam question with one of these three command terms, remember that: • If you are asked to "compare", you must write about the similarities (as opposed to "contrast" about the differences). • If you are asked to "contrast", you must write about the differences (as opposed to "compare" about the similarities).
Compare and contrast	Give an account of similarities and differences between two (or more) items or situations, referring to both (all) of them throughout.	Compare and contrast how the two managers use different planning tools to make changes to their strategies.	
Contrast	Give an account of the differences between two (or more) items or situations, referring to both (all) of them throughout.	Contrast the marketing objectives of for-profit organization X and non-profit organization Y.	

Continued on next page

Discuss	Offer a considered and balanced review that includes a range of arguments, factors or hypotheses. Opinions or conclusions should be presented clearly and supported by appropriate evidence.	Discuss whether Sam should accept the offer of a takeover. [10 marks]	This command term is frequently used in business management exam questions. There are two main reasons why many candidates do not achieve high marks: **1** Some forget to reach a clear response at the end of their answer: in the example here, the conclusion should clearly say "yes, Sam should accept the offer" or "no, Sam should not accept the offer". **2** Some start their answer with their conclusion (for example "yes, Sam should accept the offer") and then give many reasons to justify this decision. The decision, however, can only come at the very end, in the conclusion, after having reviewed all arguments and counter-arguments, all perspectives – and not at the start, as this leads to a one-sided response.
Evaluate	Make an appraisal by weighing up the strengths and limitations.	Evaluate the Bouhalbane family's decision to opt for external growth rather than internal growth.	Like the command term "discuss", the command terms "evaluate" and "examine" require you to give a balanced answer, covering both positives and negatives, strengths and limitations. This is what the examiners will do with your own exam papers: they will evaluate them, considering their strengths and limitations.
Examine	Consider an argument or concept in a way that uncovers the assumptions and interrelationships of the issue.	Examine the importance of ethics in Sofia's decision not to sell her business.	
Recommend	Present an advisable course of action with appropriate supporting evidence/reason in relation to a given situation, problem or issue.	Recommend whether *RDM* should choose Option 1 or Option 2. [10 marks]	This command term is frequently used in business management exam questions. The two main reasons why many candidates do not achieve high marks is the same as for questions with the command term "discuss": **1** Some candidates forget to reach a clear response at the end of their answer: in the example here, "*RDM* should choose Option x because there are more advantages than disadvantages". **2** Some candidates write partial answers: for example in the answer here, only about the advantages of Option 1 and the disadvantages of Option 2, which leads to a one-sided answer that lacks balance.
To what extent	Consider the merits or otherwise of an argument or concept. Opinions and conclusions should be presented clearly and supported with appropriate evidence and sound argument.	To what extent has outsourcing the manufacturing of its training provision been unsuccessful for Shailah's company	Should you have an exam question that starts with "To what extent", it is important that you follow the advice given about comparable command terms such as "discuss" and "recommend": • Consider a range of perspectives and viewpoints. • Write a balanced answer. • Reach a precise, explicit conclusion.

4. Some other command terms assess your **skills**, especially to carry out financial calculations and to construct diagrams.

Command term	Definition	Sample question	Note the following:
Annotate	Add brief notes to a diagram or graph.	Copy and annotate the product life cycle.	As part of your revision, make sure you memorize all the names and labels in the models and diagrams (for example in a break-even graph: the axes, all the lines and the break even point/quantity).
Calculate	Obtain a numerical answer showing the relevant stages in the working.	Using the information in Table 1, calculate for Location A the payback period (*show all your working*). [2 marks]	This command term is very frequently used in paper 2. Some candidates do not achieve full marks because they forget to include the unit or the percentage sign.
Complete	Add missing information/data.	Complete the profit and loss account provided.	As part of your revision, make sure you memorize the exact order of the items in the financial accounts (statement of profit and loss, statement of financial position).
Construct	Display information in a diagrammatic or logical form.	Using information from Table 1, construct the balance sheet for *Papel* for the end of October 2025. [5 marks]	This command term is frequently used in business management questions, for example about balance sheets, profit and loss accounts, cash flow forecasts or break-even charts. It is synonymous with "prepare": you may be asked to "construct" or to "prepare" a balance sheet; the task is the same.
Determine	Obtain the only possible answer.	Determine the break-even point for product X.	To determine the break-even point, you can use a graphical method or a numerical method; exam questions will usually tell you which method you should use.
Draw	Represent by means of a labelled, accurate diagram or graph, using a pencil. A ruler (straight edge) should be used for straight lines.	Draw and label a product life cycle for Strutz's No.5 jeans. [2 marks]	This command term is frequently used in business management questions, for example about product life cycle and break-even analysis.
Label	Add labels to a diagram.	Draw and label a product life cycle for Strutz's No.5 jeans. [2 marks]	This command term tends to be used together with "draw" to remind you to add key terms to a diagram such as a product life cycle or a break-even chart.
Plot	Mark the position of points on a diagram.	Plot the position of Mbarek's company on the position map drawn in your answer to part b.	This command term is commonly used when you have a visual (for example a scatter diagram or a position map); the aim is to check your ability to "read" this visual.
Prepare	Put given data or information from a stimulus/source into a suitable format.	Using the information above, prepare a fully labelled cash flow forecast for *Anubis* from January to March 2018. [2 marks]	This command term is frequently used in business management questions, for example about balance sheets, profit and loss accounts, cash flow forecasts or break-even charts. It is synonymous with "construct": you may be asked to "construct" or to "prepare" a break-even chart; the task is the same.

BUSINESS MANAGEMENT FORMULAE

In business management, we sometimes need to do calculations and apply formulae that are like mathematical equations. In your exams, those formulae will help you answer questions such as:

- calculate *XXX* profit margin for 2022 and 2023
- calculate the break-even quantity for XXX (*show all your working*)
- calculate XXX labour turnover (*show all your working*)

Most formulae are about finance, but some are about other business functions, for example about marketing (market share, market growth) or operations (break-even analysis, production planning).

Some formulae are included in the **formulae sheet** that you will receive at the start of your exams, for example profitability ratios and liquidity ratios. The first part of this section reviews them all, with extra comments to make sure that you understand how to use them.

Other formulae are **not** in the formulae sheet, so you **must** memorize them, for example formulae for break-even calculations. The second part of this section lists all these formulae.

Show all your working

means that you should not write only the final result: if you do so, you will not be awarded the maximum marks available. You must show the details of your calculation, i.e. how you reached your final result.

Formulae that are included in the formulae sheet

The **formulae sheet** includes six formulae for Standard Level and eight other for Higher Level (so 14 in total at Higher Level).

Standard Level

The six formulae at SL are the following:

Formulae	NOTE
$\text{Gross profit margin} = \dfrac{\text{gross profit}}{\text{sales revenue}} \times 100$	You calculate this **profitability ratio** by using numbers from the **statement of profit or loss**.
$\text{Profit margin} = \dfrac{\text{profit before interest and tax}}{\text{sales revenue}} \times 100$	You calculate this **profitability ratio** by using numbers from the **statement of profit or loss**. The profit margin is also sometimes called "net profit margin" in contrast to "gross profit margin".
$\text{Return on capital employed (ROCE)} = \dfrac{\text{profit before interest and tax}}{\text{capital employed}} \times 100$ where *capital employed = non-current liabilities + equity*	You calculate this **profitability ratio** by using numbers from the **statement of profit or loss** (profit before interest and tax) and from the **statement of financial position** (as both "non-current liabilities" and "equity" are found in the balance sheet).
$\text{Current ratio} = \dfrac{\text{current assets}}{\text{current liabilities}}$	You calculate this **liquidity ratio** by using numbers from the **statement of financial position** (balance sheet). You must divide current assets by current liabilities: if you calculate current assets minus current liabilities, this gives you the **working capital.**
$\text{Acid test (quick) ratio} = \dfrac{\text{current assets} - \text{stock}}{\text{current liabilities}}$	You calculate this **liquidity ratio** by using numbers from the **statement of financial position** (balance sheet).
$\text{Average rate of return (ARR)} =$ $\dfrac{(\text{total returns} - \text{capital cost}) \div \text{years of use}}{\text{capital cost}} \times 100$	The ARR measures the annual net return on an investment as a percentage of the capital cost ("capital cost" is the cost of the investment).

Higher Level

At HL, there are eight other formulae in the formulae sheet:

Formulae	NOTE
Stock turnover (number of times) $= \dfrac{\text{cost of sales}}{\text{average stock}}$ where $average\ stock = \dfrac{\text{opening stock + closing stock}}{2}$	This **efficiency ratio** can be measured and calculated in two ways: by **number of times** (this formula) and by **number of days**.
Stock turnover (number of days) $= \dfrac{\text{average stock}}{\text{cost of sales}} \times 365$ where $average\ stock = \dfrac{\text{opening stock + closing stock}}{2}$	This **efficiency ratio** can be measured calculated in two ways: by **number of days** (this formula) and by **number of times**.
Debtor days ratio (number of days) $= \dfrac{\text{debtors}}{\text{total sales revenue}} \times 365$	You calculate this **efficiency ratio** by using one number from the **statement of profit or loss** (total sales revenue) and one from the **statement of financial position** (as debtors is one of the current assets in the balance sheet).
Creditor days ratio (number of days) $= \dfrac{\text{creditors}}{\text{cost of sales}} \times 365$	You calculate this **efficiency ratio** by using one numbers from the **statement of profit and loss** (cost of sales) and from the **statement of financial position** (as creditors is one of the current liabilities in the balance sheet).
Gearing ratio $= \dfrac{\text{non-current liabilities}}{\text{capital employed}} \times 100$ where *capital employed = non-current liabilities + equity*	You calculate this **liquidity ratio** by using numbers from the **statement of financial position** (balance sheet).
Capacity utilization rate $= \dfrac{\text{actual output}}{\text{productive capacity}} \times 100$	This rate helps with production planning, the aim being to know how close a business is to the maximum capacity of 100%.
Productivity rate $= \dfrac{\text{total ouput}}{\text{total input}} \times 100$	This rate measures the productivity of a factory (or similar production unit).
Net present value (NPV) $= \sum \text{present values of return} - \text{original cost}$	The NVP is a method of **investment appraisal** based on the difference between the summation of present values of future returns and the original cost of the investment. The "present values of returns" are calculated using a **discount factor** from a **discount table** that is also provided in the exam if there is a question about NVP.

HL: How to use the discount table

The discount table looks like this:

Years	Discount rate				
	4%	6%	8%	10%	20%
1	0.9615	0.9434	0.9259	0.9091	0.8333
2	0.9246	0.8900	0.8573	0.8264	0.6944
3	0.8890	0.8396	0.7938	0.7513	0.5787
4	0.4548	0.7921	0.7350	0.6830	0.4823
5	0.8219	0.7473	0.6806	0.6209	0.4019
6	0.7903	0.7050	0.6302	0.5645	0.3349
7	0.7599	0.6651	0.5835	0.5132	0.2791
8	0.7307	0.6271	0.5403	0.4665	0.2326
9	0.7026	0.5919	0.5002	0.4241	0.1938
10	0.6756	0.5584	0.4632	0.3855	0.1615

The discount rates help you convert future cash flows to their present value; make sure you know how to read this table. For example, for a rate of 6% and for three years, you have the number 0.8396, which means that $100 invested today would only be worth (£100 x 0.8396 =) $83.96 in three years' time (because of economic factors such as inflation). To calculate VPN, you have to add all the present values (over the given number of years) and then subtract the initial investment cost. If the VPN is positive, the investment is worthwhile (see sub-unit 3.8).

Formulae that are not included in the formulae sheet

There are many other formulae that you may need for your business management exams and that are not in the formulae sheet. You **must** memorize them. They are all listed below.

Standard Level

The following two formulae (related to sub-unit 1.2) help you calculate the **profit** (for profit-making organizations) and the **surplus** (of non-profit-making organizations):

Profit = total revenues – total costs

Surplus = total revenues – total costs

The following formulae from (related to sub-unit 1.5) help explain the principles of economies of scale and diseconomies of scale, i.e. the fact that the average cost (per unit) will vary as quantity increases:

total cost = fixed cost + variable cost (TC = FC + VC)

$$\textbf{Average cost} = \frac{\text{total cost}}{\text{quantity produced}} \quad \text{or} \quad AC = \frac{TC}{Q}$$

$$AC = \frac{FC + VC}{Q}$$

This formula (related to sub-unit 2.4) helps calculate labour turnover:

$$\textbf{labour turnover} = \frac{\text{number of staff leaving over a year}}{\text{average number of staff employed in a year}} \times 100$$

These formulae (related to sub-unit 3.3) help calculate total costs and total revenue:

total costs (TC) = total fixed costs (TFC) + total variable costs (TVC).

total revenue = price per unit × quantity sold

Some formulae about final accounts are included in the formulae sheet (for example: gross profit margin and current ratio) but others are not.

These formulae (related to sub-unit 3.4) vertically follow the order of the different items of the statement of profit and loss:

- **gross profit** = sales revenue – cost of sales
- **profit before interest and tax** = gross profit – expenses
- **profit before tax** = profit before interest and tax – interest
- **profit for period** = profit before tax – tax
- **retained profit** = profit for period – dividends

In your exam, the cost of sales may not be directly given and you may have to calculate it, using the following formula:

cost of sales = opening stock + purchases – closing stock

About the statement of financial position (balance sheet) you need to know the following four formulae:

- **total assets** = non-current assets + current assets

- **total liabilities** = current liabilities + non-current liabilities

- **net assets** = total assets – total liabilities

- **equity** = share capital + retained earnings = retained earnings = net assets

To construct cash flow forecasts, remember (related to sub-unit 3.7):

profit = sales revenue – total costs

net cash flow = cash inflow – cash outflow

There are several ways to measure assessment appraisal. You can calculate the ARR (average rate of return) using the formula included in the formulae sheet. You can also calculate the payback period (measured in years and months) with the following formula (related to sub-unit 3.8):

$$\text{payback period} = \frac{\text{initial investment cost}}{\text{annual cash flow from investment}}$$

About marketing, you need to know how to calculate market share and market growth (related to sub-unit 4.1):

$$\text{market share percentage} = \frac{\text{firm's sales}}{\text{total sales in the market}} \times 100$$

$$\text{market growth percentage} = \frac{\text{market size (second year)} - \text{market size (first year)}}{\text{market size (first year)}} \times 100$$

For break even analysis, you need to know all the following formulae (related to sub-unit 5.5):

contribution per unit = price per unit – variable cost per unit

Total contribution can be calculated in two ways:

- **total contribution** = total sales revenue – total variable costs

- **total contribution** = contribution per unit × number of units sold

total revenue = price per unit × quantity sold

total costs = total fixed costs + total variable costs

Profit can be calculated in two ways:

- **profit** = total contribution – total fixed costs

- **profit** = total revenue – total costs

$$\text{break even quantity} = \frac{\text{fixed costs}}{\text{contribution per unit}}$$

margin of safety = current output – break-even quantity

$$\text{target profit output} = \frac{\text{fixed costs} + \text{target profit}}{\text{contribution per unit}}$$

$$\text{break even revenue} = \frac{\text{fixed costs}}{\text{contribution per unit}} \times \text{price per unit}$$

Higher Level

At HL, there are other formulae that you must memorize.

You need to know how to calculate depreciation; it can be done in two ways, either with the straight-line method or with the units of production method (related to sub-unit 3.4).

1. Calculating annual depreciation using the straight-line method:

$$\textbf{Annual depreciation} = \frac{\text{Original cost} - \text{residual value}}{\text{Expected useful life of asset}}$$

2. Calculating depreciation expense using the units of production method:

You start by calculating the units of production rate:

$$\textbf{units of production rate} = \left[\frac{(\text{cost basis of asset} - \text{salvage value})}{\substack{\text{estimated total units to be produced} \\ \text{over estimated useful life}}} \right]$$

which you multiply the number of units produced:

$\textbf{depreciation expense}$ = units of production rate × actual units produced

One of the pricing strategies is based on the notion of price elasticity of demand (PED); it helps measure whether a product is "price elastic" or not (i.e. how changes in its price may affect changes in demand, typically: will a higher price imply a lower demand?). The formula (related to sub-unit 4.5) to calculate PED is:

$$\textbf{price elasticity of demand} = \frac{\text{percentage change in quantity demanded } (\% \, \Delta \, \text{QD})}{\text{percentage change in price } (\% \, \Delta \, \text{P})}$$

In this equation, the sign Δ means "change". A PED below 1 is non-elastic, a PED above 1 is elastic. For example, if the price doubles (i.e. an increase of 100%) and the demand decreases by only 30% (as many people still buy this product despite the sharp increase), the PED is 0.3 which means that the product is not 'price elastic'.

With production planning, you need to know the following five formulae (related to sub-unit 5.6):

$$\textbf{defect rate} = \frac{\text{number of defective units}}{\text{total output}} \times 100$$

$$\textbf{labour productivity} = \frac{\text{total output}}{\text{total hours worked}}$$

$\textbf{working capital}$ = current assets − current liabilities

$$\textbf{working capital productivity} = \frac{\text{sales revenue}}{\text{working capital}}$$

$$\textbf{operating leverage} = \frac{\text{quantity} \times (\text{price} - \text{variable cost per unit})}{\text{quantity} \times (\text{price} - \text{variable cost per unit}) - \text{fixed costs}}$$

You also need to remember how to calculate CTB (Cost to buy) and CTM (Cost to make):

$\textbf{CTB} = P \times Q$

$\textbf{CTM} = FC + (VC \times Q)$

BUSINESS MANAGEMENT TOOLKIT

Business management toolkit

As a DP subject, business management has several components:

- topics (such as marketing and finance), summarized in units 1 to 5

- concepts (such as **ethics** and **change**), summarized in the Introduction

- tools (such as SWOT analysis and BCG matrix), summarized in this section.

Five important points about the business management toolkit:

1. The word "tool" is very broad: some of those tools are theoretical models designed by scholars (for example: Porter's Generic Forces and the Ansoff matrix), others directly come from mathematics (for example standard deviation or simple linear regression), others are the result of business practices (for example circular business models).

2. The tools are never linked to one specific sub-unit or contents element of the course. They may apply better to some business functions than others: for example, the BCG matrix is about the products that a company sells (this is called "product portfolio"), which is linked to marketing (especially the marketing mix) and operations (production planning) rather than human resources. For some tools, such as SWOT analysis and decision trees, all parts of the course are relevant.

3. You must know all the tools for all your exams, as you may have questions asking you to apply them to a particular organization.

4. You are likely to apply some of these tools in your IA (internal assessment), either as background preparation (for example a SWOT analysis or a STEEPLE analysis) or in the main body of your IA itself, as explained in the section about IA.

5. Many other tools exist in the academic subject of business management, for example Porter's 5 Forces or the VRIO framework to analyse a company's internal resources and capabilities. You will discover them if you decide to study business management at university! If you choose to write your DP extended essay in business management, you will need to research and use such tools that are beyond the syllabus (i.e. beyond the curriculum, beyond this book), but they are not necessary for your IA, nor for your exams, where you are only assessed on the course contents.

There are 16 tools in total: eight tools common for SL and HL and eight others for HL only.

Common tools for SL and HL

1. Ansoff matrix

Named after Igor Ansoff (1918-2002), the Ansoff matrix is a table that helps analyse and plan growth strategies, considering both the market (current or future) and the product (current or future). You must be able to draw it correctly, remembering the names of the four strategies (market penetration etc) and all the labels around:

		Product	
		Existing	**New**
Market	**Existing**	Market penetration	Product development
	New	Market development	Diversification

▲ **Figure 1.7.1** The Ansoff matrix

2. BCG matrix

Named after the Boston Consulting Group, this tool helps contrast and evaluate the different products sold by a company, i.e. its "product portfolio". It measures their relative market growth rate (low or high) and relative market share (low or high); they are then classified as "star", "problem child", "cash cow" or "dog". Like for the Ansoff matrix, you must remember how to draw it correctly, including the labels of the quadrants:

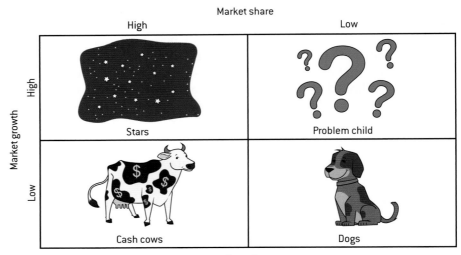

▲ **Figure 1.7.2** Boston Consulting Group (BCG) matrix

3. Business plan

A business plan is a comprehensive document where an entrepreneur outlines all the key aspects of their proposed business project. It covers the four business functions (human resources, marketing, operations and finance, especially start-up costs and the break-even point). It also includes information about the business idea itself, as well as the business's organization, aims and objectives, mission and vision statement. It is an important document for several stakeholders, especially potential shareholders and financial institutions (banks, lending companies) that may provide capital.

4. Circular business models

Circular business models are tools of sustainable development that help create a 'circular economy'. There are five main models, each with a slightly different focus:

Circular business models	Emphasis:
Circular supply model	Using renewable, recyclable or biodegradable resources as supplies (for example solar energy).
Resource recovery model	Waste is converted into raw materials for another industry (for example, instead of getting rid of food waste and agricultural waste, there are now processes to convert that organic waste into biomethane gas used to create electricity).
Product life extension model	Lengthening the lifetime of a product, before it is discarded (for example, by selling second-hand or repairing).
Sharing model	Sharing products or processes (for example carsharing (carpooling) or co-working spaces).
Product service system (PSS) model	Customers pay for the service that the product provides without the need to own the product itself (for example bicycle sharing schemes in many cities).

5. Decision trees

A decision tree is a graphical tool that uses a branching model to compare and contrast the possible outcomes of an organization's decision. The branches represent various choices, including costs, results, probabilities or risks. A decision tree provides a visual structure to help managers make decisions by mathematically identifying the most suitable outcome, from a financial viewpoint. Outcomes are typically listed as "succeed" or "fail", with a probability percentage.

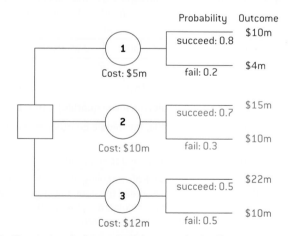

▲ **Figure 1.7.3** Example of what a decision tree looks like

The method is the following:

1. Calculate the **expected value (EV)** of the different outcomes, by multiplying the estimated outcome (expressed financially, for example $10m) by its probability (expressed as a percentage such as 80% or as a ratio such as 0.8), adding both "succeed" and "fail" scenarios for each outcome.

2. Calculate the **net gains** of each outcome (each EV minus its cost).

3. Compare the different outcomes to identify the **best expected value** which is financially the best choice.

This quantitative planning tool gives a clear answer to a complex decision, although it ignores qualitative factors that may be important.

6. Descriptive statistics

Descriptive statistics help summarize a data set by presenting a large amount of quantitative data in a simplified or manageable form. The best way to summarize a data set with a single value is to find the most representative value, the one that indicates the centre of the distribution; this is called the **central tendency**. The three most commonly used measures of central tendency are the mean, the median and the mode.

The **mean**	The sum of all values divided by the number of values (it is commonly called "the average").
The **median**	The middle value in a data set when all values are arranged in increasing order, i.e. 50% of data have a value smaller than the median and 50% of data have a value higher than the median.
The **mode**	The value that appears the most often in a data set.

To describe the dataset, it can be useful to measure the spread of the data around the central tendency: this is called a **measure of dispersion**. The most commonly used measures of dispersion are the range, the quartiles, the variance and the standard deviation.

The **range**	The difference between the highest value and the smallest value (i.e. the maximum minus the minimum).
The **quartiles**	The quartiles divide the number of data points into four parts (four quarters) of equal size: 1. The first quarter corresponds to the lowest 25% of data. 2. The second quarter corresponds to the data between 25.1% and 50% (i.e. up to the median). 3. The third quarter corresponds to the data between 50.1% to 75%. 4. The fourth quarter corresponds to the highest 25% of data. 0% 25% 50% 75% 100% | 1st quarter | 2nd quarter | 3nd quarter | 4th quarter | Q1 Q2 Q3 The number of data being (n): • Q1 (the 1st quartile, the lower quartile) = $(n + 1) \times 0.25$ • Q2 (the 2nd quartile, the middle quartile, the median) = $(n + 1) \times 0.5$ • Q3 (the 3rd quartile, the upper quartile) = $(n + 1) \times 0.75$
The **variance**	The variance is a measure of variability: it shows the degree of spread in the dataset. The more spread the data, the larger the variance is in relation to the mean. It is calculated by taking the average of squared deviations from the mean; step by step: • Calculate the mean. • Calculate each data's deviation from the mean (you will have some positive and some negative numbers). • Square each deviation from the mean (i.e. multiply each deviation from the mean by itself; this will result in only positive numbers). • Add up all of the squared deviations (this is called "the sum of squares"). • Divide the sum of squares by $n - 1$ (for a sample) or by N (for a population).
The **standard deviation**	The standard deviation (SD) is derived from variance and shows, on average, how far each value is from the mean. It's the square root of variance, calculated after the variance.

To represent large amounts of quantitative data in a simplified or manageable form, it is possible to use **pie charts** and **bar charts**:

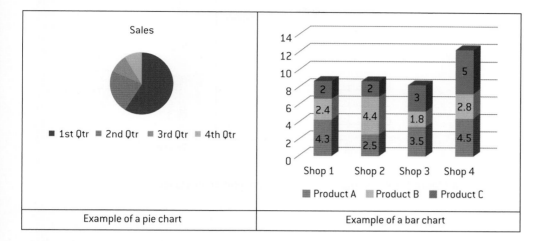

Example of a pie chart	Example of a bar chart

7. Infographics

Infographics show statistical information in a visual way that conveys key ideas, possibly combining pie charts, bar charts, numbers, images, symbols etc.

8. STEEPLE Analysis

The abbreviation STEEPLE stands for Social, Technological, Economic, Environmental, Political, Legal and Ethical. STEEPLE analysis gives a detailed overview of all the external factors that may influence an organization and therefore its decisions.

9. SWOT Analysis

The abbreviation SWOT stands for Strengths, Weaknesses, Opportunities and Threats. Strengths and weaknesses are internal aspects influencing an organization, whereas opportunities and threats are external (identified through a STEEPLE analysis). By conducting a SWOT analysis, an organization examines both internal and external factors that may have an impact on its strategic decisions.

HL only tools

HL students need to know the same tools as the SL students, as well as the following eight ones.

1. Force field analysis

A **force field analysis** (also called Lewin's model, or just abbreviated as FFA) is used to compare the driving forces and restraining forces for and against a specific strategic question, and therefore to manage change by identifying in advance where there will be resistance to change (the restraining forces). This qualitative planning tool is flexible and can be applied to many situations; however, the relative weights given to the different forces may be very subjective and hard to justify.

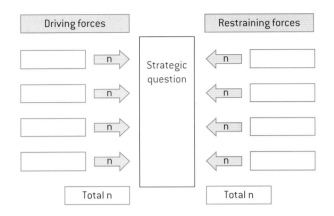

▲ **Figure 1.7.4** Example of what a force field analysis looks like

2. Gantt chart

A **Gantt chart** is used to plan a project comprised of several tasks (that may overlap), to create schedules (to manage time) and identify key deadlines (milestones). Gantt charts enable organizations to allocate resources appropriately, at the right time, and to keep an overview of the entire workflow. Presented as large tables, they give a clear picture of the progress and order of the various tasks, but they are based on estimates of the timings of each task and do not take into account important factors such as cost and quality.

	Task	Week 1	Week 2	Week 3	Week 4	Week 5	Week 6	Week 7
1	Name of task 1							
2	Name of task 2							
3	Name of task 3							
4	Name of task 4							
5	Name of task 5							
6	Name of task 6							
7	Name of task 7							

▲ **Figure 1.7.5** Example of what a Gantt chart looks like

3. Hofstede's cultural dimensions

Named after Geert Hofstede (1928-2020), this tool helps to compare and contrast the cultures of different countries. The six dimensions are: power distance, individualism/collectivism, masculinity/femininity, uncertainty avoidance, long-term/short-term orientation, indulgence/restraint. These cultural dimensions have impacts for businesses, especially for human resources management in international contexts, and for marketing, about customer behaviour, values and expectations.

4. Porter's generic strategies

Named after Michael Porter (born 1947), this tool helps identify how a business (in any industry) can obtain an advantage over its competitors (this is called "competitive advantage"). There are three generic strategies:

- **Cost leadership**

- **Differentiation**

- **Focus** (with two possibilities: cost focus and differentiation focus)

This model is visually shown by the following table, which you must memorise:

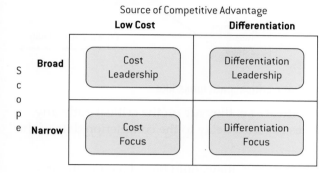

5. Contribution

Contribution is a tool to aid decision-making. It is particularly relevant for pricing and break-even analysis. You need to know the following techniques:

1. **Contribution costing** does not take indirect costs (overheads) into account. Also called 'marginal costing' and 'variable costing', it is based on the following equation that you will recognise from break-even analysis:

    Contribution (per unit) = price (charged to customer) – variable cost

2. **Absorption costing** (also called 'full costing') takes all costs into account (both direct and indirect): unlike contribution costing, it includes overheads (such as rent, insurance, security, interest on loans, office staff salaries etc), which means that more costs are included. It gives a more complete picture of the total cost of a product, but it can distort cost data (such as economies of scale).

3. **Contribution analysis** helps decide if a company should produce (make) a product, or purchase (buy) it from outside suppliers ("make or buy", see page 136):

    - If the contribution (per unit) is higher when making the product rather than buying it, the business should make it.

    - If the contribution (per unit) is higher when buying the product rather than making it, then the business should buy it.

6. Critical path analysis

Critical path analysis (CPA) is a tool used in project management. The aim is to identify the sequence (order) of tasks, the timings and interdependencies of each activity (for example if one must be completed before another one starts), and the minimum duration required to complete the entire project (especially when different stages overlap). It helps set rational deadlines and monitor progress.

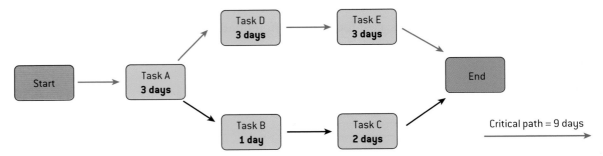

▲ **Figure 1.7.6** Example of what a critical path looks like

- Some activities are "**critical**" i.e. they are on the critical path: any delay in those activities causes a delay to the completion date of the project.

- Some activities have "**float**" i.e. they could be delayed without causing a delay to the overall project. There is a distinction between:

    - The "**total float**": the amount of time an activity can be delayed from its early start date without delaying the entire project.

    - The "**free float**": the amount of time an activity can be delayed without delaying the early start date of the next activity.

7. Simple linear regression

This set of mathematical tools helps describe or predict the relationship between two variables, estimating how changes in an independent variable affect changes in the dependent variable. You need to know how to construct and interpret a **scatter diagram** (also called scatter plot, scatter chart, scatter graph) with the **line of best fit** (also called trend line) showing **correlation** and **extrapolation**.

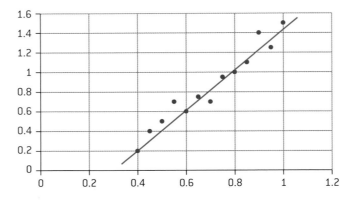

▲ **Figure 1.7.7** Example of a scatter diagram with the line of best fit showing a positive correlation

Index